Who's Th

THE TRUE STORY OF

A LEEDS HAUNTING

Who's There?

THE TRUE STORY OF
A LEEDS HAUNTING

Colette Shires

The
History
Press

To my niece Amanda, 18 July 1961 – 28 May 2005

First published 2008

The History Press Ltd
The Mill, Brimscombe Port
Stroud, Gloucestershire, GL5 2QG
www.thehistorypress.co.uk

British Library Cataloguing in Publication Data.
A catalogue record for this book is available from the
British Library.

ISBN 978 07524 4808 4

Typesetting and origination by The History Press Ltd.
Printed in Great Britain

CONTENTS

	Introduction	6
	My Immediate Family	7
1	Moving House	8
2	The First Signs	13
3	The Haunting	19
4	The Ghosts	31
5	Tony	39
6	Homeless	44
7	A New Start	52
8	The House in Potternewton	59
9	The Accident	67
10	The Ghosts of Oakwood Hall	77
11	Dad	81
12	The Hollies	87
13	The Croft	93

INTRODUCTION

I would be a very wise woman indeed if I could give cut and dried answers to explain the existence of ghosts. Psychic research has endeavoured for years to provide them.

I am not offering proof of their existence, but a true, unexaggerated account of the many paranormal events that took place in the homes of my parents. It is for you to make your own judgement of the existence of ghosts by assessing the strange phenomenon that occurred.

I know some people think I am slightly unhinged when I tell them I believe in ghosts. And who could blame them? Ghosts are not exactly the normal, everyday things they are likely to come across, but for my family, friends, and me for years they were almost part of our everyday life.

Apart from my mother, who few believed, and my ex sister-in-law, who spilled the beans, we were reluctant to speak about the haunted house other than to a selected few. For quite some time, we even found it difficult to discuss our strange experiences amongst ourselves. As I have grown older, however, I have become braver and wiser, and the way I see it now is that, no matter what others say or think, I cannot alter this part of my life, and the fact that I was there and lived it. Therefore, other people's opinions do not affect me like they once did. I am just a normal, every day person. So much has happened: it is a story that must be told, and I want to tell it because I do not *think* ghosts exist – I *know* they do!

MY IMMEDIATE FAMILY

My parents

Edna Slater (*née* Walters)
Arthur Slater

My brothers and sisters (from the eldest to the youngest)

Laura
Alfred
Edmond
Brideen
Myself – Colette
Conrad

One

MOVING HOUSE

My story begins in the early summer of 1958, when I was almost eleven years old and we were to leave Glover Street because my mother could no longer face living there. Everything had changed after the deaths of her ageing parents. Her mother passed away first from cancer in 1952; then, two years later, her father followed. Mamma always said he died of a broken heart. She missed them terribly, and now the rest of her family was moving away from the area, so she wanted to move too.

My parents, Edna and Arthur Slater, had spent months scouring the city of Leeds trying to find a suitable property in the right place at the right price and size. The ideal location in my mother's mind would be as near as possible to the city centre because she would consider herself as living in the back of beyond if she was not in walking distance of the shops. With a husband and children to shop for, the nearer the shops were to her doorstep, the better.

As it was for most people at that time, we did not possess a car. I cannot recall of ever thinking we had a need for one, as trams and buses were plentiful. My mother usually walked into town, but sometimes caught a tram or bus home if she was heavily laden with groceries. She loved the hustle and bustle of city life, and would never have dreamed for a moment of living in the country; she loved the country, but only for its beauty and as a holiday destination. My father was very easy going, and would go along with whatever she wanted. He was able to settle wherever he could throw his cap. This was the longest they had lived in the same house since the war, so to them another move was no big issue.

My older sister Brideen had the job of taking Conrad (my younger brother) and me to see our new home for the first time. She was fifteen years old then. I can still see us now. It was Saturday. Mamma had made sure that none of us were to visit the house empty-handed. Conrad and I were loaded up with our bits and pieces, carrying them on our way like busy little ants. Brideen was leading, a big cloth bag thrown over her shoulder. Her once long, blond hair, now cropped short, made her look even taller than before. A weak glimmer of sun managed to shine through the overcast sky adding an extra glow to her natural fairness. Brideen and Conrad, being fairer than me, took after the Slater's side of the family.

My older sister, Brideen.

I was darker and brown eyed and took after the Walters' side. As I walked up the road swinging a very full brown paper bag, the handles made from thin strings cut into my fingers creating deep grooves close to the bone, but that did not dampen my enthusiasm. Even though I did not want to leave our old house, I still felt excited with the idea of living somewhere else. I was confused with my feelings, but the reality of it was I wanted the best of both worlds, which I could not have, so I looked upon the move as an adventure with a lot of exploring to look forward to.

Although the house was only a mile or so from our old home, the area was unfamiliar to me. I had only ever passed through it on the tram to Roundhay Park before. Now they had buses instead.

'Will I have to catch a bus to school, Brideen?'

'No, it's just a little bit further than before; you'll just go a different way.'

I had hoped the answer would be yes as I always wanted to go to school by bus. Noisily, we walked on, chattering and pointing out this and that. We bombarded Brideen with our questions about the house and the area.

'Wait and see,' she answered repeatedly with a big grin across her face. Her green eyes flashed at our impatience. 'We'll soon be there. It's not far.'

We crossed over Sheepscar, a triangular-shaped intersection, and turned off to walk along Roundhay Road. We passed a library, pubs, shops, and streets of terraced houses, some back to backs. Eventually, we approached a schoolyard surrounded by wrought-iron railings. The school building was set back at the bottom of the yard which sloped away

Looking down Roundhay Road – what was Grant Street is behind the railings on the right.

from the busy main road. Looking through the railings and across the yard, we could see a row of old terraced houses. They were larger than the other houses we had seen – taller somehow. Brideen pointed her finger towards them.

'Look, the sixth one down is ours,' she said.

'It's not one of those back to backs, is it?'

'No, Colette. They are all through houses sort of like our old one, except they don't have a garden at the back, just a small yard.'

'I've been here already,' piped up Conrad. 'Mamma brought me with her to see it.'

'Where had I been?' I wondered. Everyone seemed to have seen the house except me. I did not feel a need for a garden at my age then, so I did not mind not having one. So far everything met with my approval – until we reached the house. On seeing it close to I could not help but feel a little disappointed in it. It seemed to loom over us, yet it was not any larger than the house we were about to leave. It was built of traditional red brick. It had a tiny garden at the front, and not much of a view looking across the school playground to the street opposite. There was no extended family in sight. The address was No. 11 Grant Street at the front and No. 12 Grant Place at the back.

It was obvious that the house had not been decorated for many years, outside or in. The wallpaper and paint work were the drabbest I had ever seen. I thought that perhaps it was the awful décor that put me off, and I had to admit to myself that our old house was much nicer.

Dad in Grant Street, taken
from outside No. 11.

I decided then that I really did not want to move here. I wanted to stay in Glover Street
where I was happy. I could not understand why my parents chose this house to buy: I
could only guess that they took it on purely out of frustration because they had difficulties
in finding a house that they really wanted and were sick and tired of looking around. I
don't know why they finally chose this house in Grant Street, other than it being near
enough to town.

Dad and our two elder brothers Alfred and Edmond (named after Dad's brothers)
were already at the house when we arrived. They were doing the preparations
for redecorating. They only had the weekends and evenings to do so as they were all
busy with their day jobs. My father was a pipe fitter at the time. Alfred, the eldest of
the two, worked on the buildings as a hod carrier, and Edmond was a roofer. Even a
stranger would know that they were brothers as they were very much alike, same good
physique, and thick dark hair, and both good-looking enough to break a girl's heart.
They took after the Walters' side of the family in looks. They did not have time to chat
to us, so we just got on with scouting the bare large square rooms with Brideen acting as
our guide. She told us that on her previous visits she'd heard the sounds of a baby's cry

coming from somewhere upstairs. Knowing that there was no baby around, not even next door, she came to the conclusion that she must have mistaken the cries of a cat for a baby as they could sound very much alike at times, and she had no other explanation. She had already searched the entire house, but could not find anything and assumed that the 'cat' had to be trapped somewhere in the house out of sight, perhaps between the floorboards or up a chimneybreast. On hearing this, the three of us began a search for the 'trapped cat'. As the house was not yet furnished, it should be easy to find, especially now that there were three of us to look for it. Our stampeding footsteps echoed up the uncarpeted stairs and around the house. We hunted from the cellar to the attic, but found nothing. Later, we were in the kitchen eating fish and chips for lunch when I heard it.

'Shush. Listen!'

Sitting very still with full mouths and eyes wide we stared at each other as the sad cries drifted down the stairs from somewhere in the bedrooms. We got up and moved to the foot of the stairs and listened carefully. The cat did indeed sound just like a baby. Feeling confident that we should definitely find it this time as we could go directly to its source, we went up to the bedrooms to resume our search. But the cries hung in the air as they met our ears and made it very difficult to judge from which direction they came. We put our ears to the floors and walls, looked and listened up the chimney breasts, but to no avail. We could not find the poor unfortunate creature anywhere. I felt that the strange sounds may have come from a space beneath the attic stairs, but it was impossible for anything to be there and not be found. Defeated, we gave up the search.

Off and on for the next two weeks, the crying continued to be heard around the house before eventually falling silent. We could only guess that the 'cat' had died. We felt very sad and unhappy at not being able to help it. We were not to know then that the crying would be heard a number of times over the years to follow.

The day came for us to move in. Everyone seemed to be happy about it and their enthusiasm soon brushed off onto me. My disappointment had quickly dispersed after the house had been decorated and furnished. It looked so much more presentable. I began to feel excited again. We moved in without any problems.

Brideen and I shared the large attic bedroom. We thought it would be great, thinking that we would have a better view of the moon and stars. The reality was that it was as black as pitch when the light was out because the streetlights did not reach the skylight window. I still liked it though, because it was well away from the rest of the house and I could play records without disturbing anyone. The room had been decorated in lovely, yellow, 'Madam Butterfly' wallpaper. It looked bright and sunny, but it did not take long for the walls to be plastered with pop pin-ups, mainly of Elvis Presley. Everyone else slept in the rooms on the floor below.

Two

THE FIRST SIGNS

A year or so later, Dad made and fitted a new door in the kitchen to close off a tiny hall leading to the stairs and the sitting room. During the school summer holidays, I was surprised to be given the job of painting the door by Mamma. While I carefully applied an undercoat, she busied herself outside with the washing and tidying up the yard, but made sure she checked up on me every few minutes, filling me with praise for doing a good job. Then she called out, 'Colette, come and look at this on the wall!' I looked up to see my mother's face come into view as she pushed open the back door and beckoned me outside.

'Just a second.'

I carefully laid the paintbrush across the top of the tin before getting up from my knees. Then I headed out of the house. Mamma was standing by the gate and poking her finger at the wall.

'Look!' she said, before I'd even got down the steps to the yard. As I got closer, my eyes followed her finger and focused on some crude engravings on the yard wall. They were difficult to see at first, as they were as black as the rest of the stone around them, making it obvious that they had been there for many years. (It was normal in those days for everything to be blackened by sooty smoke as it billowed from coal fires, especially in a large industrial city such as Leeds). They were symbols of some sort.

'What are they?' I asked.

'Oh! Colette, they look like black magic or something. What do you think?' Even though I was still a child, she often respected my opinion, which made me feel quite responsible and grown up.

'I don't know,' I answered truthfully, and ran my fingers over the strange shapes. But I had seen something like them before, perhaps in a film or comic book.

'Do you really think they could be black magic things, Mam?'

'Oh, God! I hope not,' she said in a low voice.

'... Mam...What *is* black magic?'

'Ooh! It's Devil worship – the occult and things.'

I had heard of Devil worship and the occult, but I had never come across anything relating to it before. We were intrigued by the strange markings. They seemed to hold some sort of symbolic significance, but we were baffled as to who made them and why.

I was back at school after the holiday and returned home one day to find my mother trying to chisel out the strange shapes. Her curiosity for them had slowly built up to a strong dislike.

'What are you doing?' I asked.

She turned and looked at me as I walked through the gate. Her hair was covered in fragments of stone, which somehow looked comically out of place with the serious expression on her face.

'I'm getting rid of this. It does not belong around a Catholic household. I think it has got something to do with black magic, so I don't want it here.'

I did not know what to make of it. As she chiselled, the light sandstone underneath began to show through.

'But look what you're doing to the wall. You are making it look very messy.'

'I don't give a hang!' she said. 'I just want to get rid of it. I'm going to cement it over.'

I left her to it and went into the house. After I put my things away, I went into the front room to play the piano. As I raised the lid, I heard my mother's voice call out.

'Colette! Oh, Colette!' She sounded distressed. Her voice was almost like a scream. I jumped up from the piano stool and raced out to her.

'What's the matter?'

'Look at this!' she said as I appeared in the open doorway. She turned and pointed to the wall. I ran down the steps from the house to take a closer look, and was shocked at what I saw. The face of horned goat was clearly looking out at us. It had not been there before.

'It's a ram's head. It's a ram's head,' said Mamma.

'Are you sure you didn't do it?'

'No, I couldn't do that. I was only making a rough surface for the cement to grip.'

With no further ado, with cement already mixed, she quickly plastered over it.

'There now, it's gone,' she said softly, as if reassuring herself. But that was not the end of it. A few days later the cement fell out. The ugly defacement stared out at us once again. Mamma re-chiselled and re-cemented it several times thereafter, but it still fell out – and the face seemed to become more apparent each time. After a long time, some of the cement eventually stayed in place, but to cover only half the face. Mamma quickly grew to hate the house and stayed out of it as much as she could.

By the time I reached thirteen years of age I had settled quite well into the house. I had not given Glover Street much thought, as it now seemed an age ago, as did the crying cat and the markings on the yard wall. But I was to wonder about the carvings once more when I was standing in the front doorway of the house, looking out on to the tiny front garden and street. Alfred had cemented the frontage of the house giving it a stone effect, which smartened up the old brickwork considerably.

Three people walked by: a middle-aged man, a woman and a girl aged around eight years old. My mother had also spotted them, and whispered into the back of my neck that they were the family who had lived in the house before us.

The woman, possibly in her late thirties, looked miserable and kept her eyes straight ahead. The little girl, holding her hand, did not take her eyes from the ground as they walked by. Neither of them gave the house or me the slightest hint of a glance. I thought this was rather odd. I would have found it almost impossible to keep such a restraint on my natural curiosity, yet even the little girl could do it. The man did look across, and gave me a small, smarmy smile. I disliked him instantly. I felt as if he was looking down on me, and thought how cheeky of him to do so, considering that he had left the house in such a drab state. And for some unexplained reason, I wondered in the back of my mind if he had been responsible for the carvings on the wall.

'I don't like the look of those people,' I said to my mother after they had passed by. She glanced after them through the window, and then spoke out loud. 'Yes, I know what you mean; I thought they were strange too.'

That was the first and last time I ever saw or heard of them.

One evening, towards the Christmas of 1959, my family and I were quietly watching television in the living room. Victor, our curly haired, Airedale-terrier cross, was lying under a chair. He was an intelligent and obedient dog and we all loved him. A big coal fire roared in the grate and we all sat snuggled into the settee and armchairs that surrounded it. It was a cosy, tranquil scene.

Suddenly, Victor startled us by scrambling madly out from under the chair. It clattered as it was tossed to one side by his body. He was frantic, and without warning he charged across the room as if propelled. To our amazement, he leaped into the air and began a frenzied attack at some unknown entity in the space between the top of the door and the ceiling. He was in a rage like we had never seen before. Keeping his eyes fixed firmly on the spot, he frantically tried to reach whatever it was by leaping off the back of the settee and biting into the air. He then found he could reach the space better by jumping off a nearby chair instead, but again, he just bit the air. We had never seen him act so viciously, and sat with our mouths wide open at his unusual behaviour. After the initial shock we attempted to calm him, but he would have none of it. The door from the living room led to the tiny hall in the centre of the house and to the bedroom stairs. We searched the house upstairs and downstairs, inside and out in a vain attempt to find a reason for his outburst. Our efforts did not satisfy him, and we were unable to distract him from the space above the door. We passed our hands through the space in an effort to show him that there was nothing there, but this only made him more intent on attack. Eventually, after a lot of coaxing, he retreated briefly from his solitary fight, but only to repeat the scenario all over again.

The evening pressed on and Victor calmed a little. He went back to lie under the now straightened chair, but his eyes never left the spot above the door. He continued to growl and snarl. We all sat quietly with our own thoughts, afraid to say what we were thinking – either that Victor had gone mad and would have to be put down, or there was something very strange in this room with us that only Victor could see!

The following day we were relieved to see that Victor was his normal loveable self again. He never repeated his odd behaviour of the night before, and continued his life as any normal dog would.

Even though all my instincts told me that Victor did see something in the room that evening, I did not consider at that time that the house might be haunted. I suppose it was because I did not know what to expect from a haunted house. I took the incident to be a one off, weird event.

A few months after the incident with Victor, Mamma confided in me that she was very worried about my brother, Alfred. I was only going on thirteen years old but she must have thought I was mature enough to understand. 'You're sensible,' she'd say – though I don't know what gave her that idea! I would think to myself, 'Surely I would have done better at school and other things if that was true.' Alfred was the apple of my mother's eye: she always told me what a good son he was to her, and how as a little boy he often helped her out. Being ten years my senior and working, he gave Conrad and me pocket money now and again, although he often teased us too.

'I'm worried about his nerves,' said Mamma. 'I think he's heading for a nervous breakdown.'

'Why's that?' I felt a knot tighten in my stomach.

'He told me that he is seeing things, and asked if he should go to the doctor.'

Now I felt sick. To me, Alfred was someone who worked hard and enjoyed life, but always kept a level head on his shoulders. I could not conceive the idea that there could be anything wrong with his nerves.

'What did he see?'

'He told me that he'd seen a girl with long dark hair, aged ten or so, walk past him through the kitchen, then make her way upstairs to the bedrooms.'

'Who was she?'

'He didn't know. He assumed she had walked in from the street and was shocked at her cheek. He told her to "come back here", but she ignored him and walked into my bedroom.'

'Then what?'

'He followed her into the room, but she wasn't there. No one was there.' Mamma turned away from me as she continued. 'This gave him a shock and puzzled him. He didn't say anything about it to anyone. That was, until a second, equally strange incident occurred that prompted him to tell me.'

'What was that?'

'It was last Saturday lunchtime. Everyone was out except him. He was sitting at the kitchen table eating a sandwich. He sensed something, which made him turn around and look towards the cellar door. He was horrified to see a man quietly standing there, watching him. Then the man laughed at him before fading away a few moments later, leaving a void beside the door.'

'Did he say what the man looked like?'

'He said he had a small, pointed beard, wore strange clothes and a peculiar hat. What do you think if it, Colette? Do you think his nerves are bad?'

'He seems okay to me, Mam; had he been drinking at all?'

'No!'

My poor brother. I was upset to hear all this. I could not imagine for one moment that there might be something wrong with him. I could understand my mother's anguish. I was not sure as to what I could do to help him, if anything. I settled to watching him closely. He must have noticed the extra attention that I was giving him, but if he did, he did not say so.

My brother Alfred.

He appeared to be quite normal to me. I could not see anything amiss with him – and indeed he was normal, for as time went by it became clear that it was the house at fault, and not my brother.

Laura, our eldest sister, left home whilst we were still living in Glover Street. She was on the stage. She danced, acted, and modelled, doing whatever work came her way. But this meant that she spent most of her time travelling. She was small, very good-looking with long dark hair and big brown eyes. She had a son, Gary, who spent most of his time in the care of my mother. He was more like a little brother than a nephew to us.

One summer evening, when he was about six years old, Gary had been put to bed. He was never any trouble at bedtime and always went quite willingly. Therefore, around nine-thirty, we were alarmed to hear his screams coming from upstairs. My mother, Conrad and I charged up to his bedroom fearing that something was terribly wrong. It was still twilight, and we could see easily into the bedroom as we opened the door. Gary was sitting on his pillow, cowering and crying. He looked at us through tear-filled eyes. Between sobs, he told us that a man had wakened him. 'He was leaning over me and laughed – right into my face,' he said. Gary described the man as having a little beard and wearing a funny hat! To our knowledge, no one had mentioned Alfred's sighting of a strange man to Gary; he was much too young, yet his description of him was the same. This little episode and other small incidents convinced me that Alfred's encounter with the laughing man had not been his imagination playing tricks on him after all.

It did not take long thereafter to establish the fact that the house was haunted. So many minor, unexplained incidents frequently happened to us at various times of day or night. It was not unusual to be tapped on the head or shoulder when no one was near, or even to get a dig in the back. Bumping into something large and solid but invisible was very common.

Sometimes, just before entering the front room, I would hear the piano keys being gently brushed against, even when the lid was closed. On hearing the keys, I would quickly put my head around the door in an attempt to catch the musician out, but I never could. Often, in the dead of night, I would be woken out of a deep sleep by a heavy weight landing with a thud on my bed. Terrified and unable to relax, I'd stiffly lie still until the thing eventually dispersed. On occasions, I would turn over and bump into it as it sat on my bed beside me. Sometimes it would be at the foot of my bed, restricting me from stretching out my legs. It was heavy and as solid as a brick wall. It was a terrible experience to encounter in the middle of the night, alone in one's bed.

My mother often remarked that when she was standing by the kitchen table, she would feel a sensation of something like a cat wrapping itself around her ankles and passing between them. She had almost tripped over it on occasions, but could never see anything to account for it. On other occasions she said she'd heard a steady tap… tap… tap from under her bed, which she could only describe as being like a stick hitting the floor and the underside of the bed itself. During one particular night, the noise disturbed my father, who was lying in the bed beside her. Half asleep and thinking he was dreaming, he asked my mother, 'Why are the children under the bed in the middle of the night, Edna?' Somehow he had overlooked the fact that we were no longer small enough to fit under the bed, let alone have the inclination to play under there in the middle of a cold dark night. 'What children?' She asked him. 'Have you forgotten that we don't have small children any more?'

The following morning, he had no recollection of asking about the children under the bed, but complained about all the noise that was going on. The reason for the tapping was never to be discovered.

Another night, Mamma and I were abruptly awakened by a terrifically loud bang. My immediate thought was that it came from my parent's bedroom. I leaped out of bed and dashed to them, thinking that something was seriously wrong. I was under the impression that the whole window, frame and all, had somehow blown out. I had a horrible thought that my mother or father may have fallen through it. I met my mother at her bedroom door as she came rushing out: she was on her way to my room as she felt sure that the noise came from there. Through her bedroom door I was relieved to see my father still sleeping. I wondered how on earth he remained undisturbed. Mamma and I quietly searched the house, room by room, taking care not to wake anyone. We were amazed to find everyone, even Victor, still fast asleep. Although we were both convinced that the noise came from inside the house, we continued our search outside. Everything was intact and silent. The next morning we checked with neighbours to see if they had heard anything, but drew a blank. We found it so hard to believe that no one else had heard it. The whole thing remained a complete mystery to us.

As well as inexplicable noises to contend with, items were going missing, even from locked drawers. They were not usually things of great value, and, more often than not, they were small objects. Sometimes they would reappear, taking up to a year to do so; on other occasions they were never seen again. These, and other small incidents that occurred, did not amount to much on their own, but collectively, there was a lot of unexplained activity going on in the house.

Three

THE HAUNTING

By the time I was fourteen years old, Alfred and Edmond had both married and left home. At the age of seventeen, Brideen had joined the Army, much to the dismay of our parents. They did not like the idea of her leaving home at such a young age, but she was strong willed and determined and managed to convince them that it was the best thing for her. Indeed, it later turned out to be a successful move: Army life suited her very well, and most of all, she was happy.

In those days, my father was a civil servant employed by the Department of the Environment. His work took him around the country where he installed and maintained heating systems and the like in government buildings. He did this for years, but managed to return home for most weekends. Never before did our home feel so empty of family. Because we had always been used to a full house, the emptiness was quite noticeable to us who were left – Mamma, Conrad, myself and Gary.

Edmond and his wife, Sandra, had a setback with a house that they were hoping to move into. This caused serious problems for them. By this time they had a baby girl, my niece, Amanda. They were forced to move to temporary accommodation, which was far from suitable for them. So my mother came to their aid and offered them the use of our front room and the bedroom above it until they could sort things out. They took up the offer and moved in. As my mother was afraid of being in the house alone, she was pleased to have the company of Sandra during the day.

We generally kept quiet about the 'ghosts' to the outside world. It was not the sort of thing that rational people spoke about. My mother, however, did mention the odd word to one or two people, including our family doctor, who, not surprisingly, did not believe her stories about the house and could not understand why she was so frightened of it. He treated her for bad nerves.

It was inevitable that the time would come when we would have to face the fact that the house was haunted; we could not go on pretending otherwise – the mounting evidence was eliminating any traces of doubt that we may have had. The time did arrive when we were unable to keep it under wraps any longer, after Sandra unintentionally brought the haunting to the attention of our neighbours. It did not take long for Sandra to feel that the house was 'not quite right'. She too was to discover the strange affliction it held within its walls, something she had never felt or known before.

One afternoon my mother was sweeping the pavement outside the house and chatting to neighbours as they passed by. All at once, they were distracted by the sounds of Sandra's screams ripping through the air from inside the house. A moment later, the knob on the back door rattled and the door was flung open. Sandra, still screaming and in a panic, fled from the house into the street and ran to my mother's side. 'Something is on the stairs!' she screamed, flapping her hands like some kind of strange bird.

On hearing the commotion, people came out of their houses to see what all the fuss was about. Sandra told them. 'I was climbing the stairs. I was about half way up when something blocked my way. I bumped into it because I could not see it. It was big and solid and almost knocked me off my feet, but I still could not see anything.' So there it was – the cat had been let out of the bag. A short exchange then took place as Mamma tried to explain the haunting to the shocked neighbours; the secret was out.

Mamma led the way back into the house with Sandra following behind and the neighbours looking on. She knew 'it' was not likely to still be on the stairs, but nevertheless she gingerly entered and glanced over her shoulder at the array of bewildered faces. Then, quietly, she closed the door.

Another time, Sandra, Mamma and baby Amanda were two doors away in a neighbour's house. Unknown to them, Sandra's mother, Mrs Shepherd, had arrived to pay her daughter a visit. As usual, the back door that led straight into the kitchen was left unlocked, so she entered. When she pushed open the door she heard the cries of a baby, and, unsurprisingly, believed it to be Amanda. The cries were coming from the front sitting room. She called out to Sandra, fully expecting her to be there with Amanda. But there was no answer. She called out again, and still there was no reply. By now she had become angry because she thought Amanda had been left alone in the house and experienced acute fears that all was not well. The crying became louder as she headed for the sitting room. The door was ajar, so she pushed it slightly and looked in. At the far side of the room, she could see Amanda's pram with the hood up. She could not see inside it yet as it was facing away from her, but the crying became louder. She went straight to the pram and peered inside – and the crying stopped instantly. To her astonishment and disbelief, the pram was empty. She turned and ran from the house.

A number of other weird incidents happened whilst Edmond and Sandra were staying at the house. At night, they were frequently disturbed by something playing with the toys inside Amanda's toy box. Mamma had the idea to sprinkle flour on the floor around it to see if any prints would be left, but the flour was never disturbed.

In the early hours of one morning, Edmond was awakened by something gripping him by the throat. He could only assume that it was Sandra trying to kill him, and wondered what terrible thing he'd done wrong for her to do such a thing. He struggled and elbowed her to make her stop – and found that the bed beside him was empty. He was just able to see across the darkened room, dimly lit from a yellow glow of a street lamp outside, and made out Sandra standing by the window, looking out. She was crying.

My niece Amanda in the front room of the house in Grant Street.

He knew then that it was not she trying to asphyxiate him – but who was? There was nobody near him. He could not understand how this was happening to him.

Sandra was totally unaware of his predicament and continued to look out of the window, weeping. Suddenly the choking stopped. Edmond's eyes opened wider to scan the room in search of a reason for his horrific experience, but could see nothing to account for it.

'What's wrong? Why are you crying?' He asked her in a rasping voice.

'I'm frightened of this house,' she replied.

He declined to question her any further; he was too terrified himself, and did not want to tell her what had just happened to him as she was troubled enough already.

Only a few nights later, when they were both snuggled up in bed, their cosiness was disturbed when they heard clawing and scratching noises coming from beneath the bedroom window inside the room. They were too afraid to move or turn on the light to see what was causing it. They did not dare speak. Horrified, they just laid there in the darkness and listened. After what seemed an eternity, it stopped. The next morning when they looked at the wall they found the wallpaper ripped to shreds.

Another time, it was three o'clock in the afternoon. I had only just got in the door after running an errand for my mother. She was peeling onions in preparation for our dinner, which we always had early on a Saturday. She smiled but did not speak as I thrust the shopping towards the kitchen table. Sandra was mixing something in a bowl. She turned her head towards me and asked, 'Will you fetch Amanda down for me please, Colette?

I think she's awake.' Amanda was around eighteen months old and usually took an afternoon nap. I went up to the bedroom to fetch her.

Before I entered the room I heard her laughter coming from inside. I smiled and walked in to see her sitting on the bed. She beamed a big smile in return, which quickly turned into a gleeful laugh. She was a pretty, happy child and never seemed to cry much. 'Come on Amanda, time to come down,' I said and reached out to pick her up, but she pushed my hands away.

'Baby,' she said, and pointed her small chubby finger to the foot of the bed. I looked to see an empty space, and all at once, goose pimples erupted on my body and a creeping sensation ran up my scalp. I always felt this when a ghost was present. 'There's no baby,' I told her. I began to feel frightened: my senses told me that something was there, even though I could not see anything. 'Baby, baby,' Amanda repeated continuously. She darted forward with her little arm outstretched to reach for it. I grabbed her to hold her back. She became very annoyed with me and with great determination, she tried to fight me off, and her laughter became shrieks. As the situation developed, the now familiar sensation of my hair rising like the hackles on a dog's back became stronger, accompanied by a strange coldness. I was now convinced that something other than Amanda was on the bed, but in spite of being in no doubt that something was there, I felt silly for being so frightened of it. I snatched Amanda up into my arms and hurried downstairs to safety. I guessed that the look on my face and Amanda's cries to go back upstairs told Sandra and Mamma that something was amiss. They understood and fearfully accepted the situation when I explained to them what had just happened. Amanda frequently encountered the 'baby' thereafter.

Edmond with Amanda (sitting down) and baby Darren in his arms.

Before moving on and into their own home, Sandra and Edmond discovered they were expecting their second child, who was to be my nephew, Darren. Before his birth, Sandra had been buying and storing baby clothes in a chest of drawers in the bedroom, using the largest bottom drawer. The new clothes were neatly placed in it and kept in their original wrappers to await the day they would be needed. When that day arrived, Mamma went to fetch them. On opening the drawer, the smile slid from her face – the drawer was completely empty. Although there was nothing to be seen, I watched as her hands fumbled along the base of the drawer as she stared in disbelief at the empty space. Her eyes and mind could not comprehend that the clothes were gone. We searched the rest of the drawers, hoping that they had been moved, but to no avail.

After Sandra and Edmond had moved out the bedroom was unoccupied for a year or more, and the chest of drawers remained unused. Mamma had bought some new sheets and decided to store them in the drawers. She opened the drawer that once contained the baby clothes and was astonished to find them returned to it, just as they had been left, wrappers and all. But now, as almost a year had gone by since their disappearance, they were too small for Darren to wear! This was just one of many odd things that would happen in the house. Another was a chiming clock that disappeared from the mantelpiece for almost two days. One morning we all got up to find it back in its original place keeping perfect time. No one had seen it go or return.

We were never quite sure if 'our' ghost or ghosts always hung around the house. Occasionally something would happen to make us think otherwise. Here are examples of times when we believe they left the house.

Laura sometimes managed to get a small part in the odd film. Mamma was very proud of her and would drop everything to go and see her on the big screen if she could. My first real job at the age of fifteen was nowhere near as glamorous, at the C.W.S. shoe manufactures as a trainee shoemaker, but I enjoyed it all the same. One dark, late autumn evening, I had only been home from work for about two minutes when Mamma pulled on her coat and darted off to the cinema. She'd discovered only half an hour before that a documentary film called *That's Life*, in which Laura was appearing, had been showing in Leeds all the week and this evening, as it was Friday, was the final showing. The old Yorkshire saying 'There's nowt so queer as folk' comes to mind when I recall that evening. Conrad and I were the only two people in the house. Around seven o'clock, a loud knocking and pounding disturbed us as it bounced off the back door. We were not expecting anyone, but whoever it was his – or her – heavy-handed manner sounded threatening to us. I cautiously opened the door to find two scowling, rather large women standing in the yard near to the back steps. I had never seen them before, but quickly decided that they must be sisters, as they looked so much alike.

'Is this the haunted house?' The larger of the two women demanded. I was quite taken aback by her question and wished my mother were home. 'Well, err… yes! I suppose it is,' I answered carefully. 'Why do you want to know?' The other woman, who I took to be the youngest, stepped forward and yelled: 'Because 'your' ghost has moved into my house!' She jabbed a finger towards some house further down the street. She must have been a new occupier, and I wondered how she could have known about the ghosts. 'Nothing wrong, I hope!' I asked with a tongue like slush, not knowing what else to say. She did not reply.

Instead, the larger and older of the two, who I guessed to be in her late thirties, moved further into the light shining out from the open doorway. She was angry and began to shout at me, her arms waving in the air as she ranted on. I managed to make out that she was complaining that 'our' ghost had banged so hard on their bedroom floor that it caused plaster to fall from the ceiling below it and caused a light fitting to swing about. I had never come across a situation like this before, and did not know how to respond. For a few moments I felt really lost. I could only stand there, staring at the women whilst Conrad looked on over my shoulder.

'I'll tell my mother when she comes in,' I managed to say in a weak voice.

'What time will that be?' The older woman snapped.

'I don't know, she's gone to the pictures.'

'Pictures, pictures,' she mimicked, and then added, 'We'll be back!'

With that, the two women stormed off in a huff and I shut the door.

Out loud, I asked myself, 'What was I supposed to do? Tell the ghost not to be naughty and come back home?' This remark tickled Conrad's sense of humour then latched on to mine, and, in seconds, we were both crying with laughter.

Later, when Mamma returned home, she confirmed that the women had recently moved into the street. She had no idea who had told them about the ghosts. She was also lost for words when I told her what had happened and laughed at the idea of it. I never saw the two women again, but heard later that they had moved away.

I was a member of the Junior Legion of Mary at the Holy Rosary church, where we would meet for one evening a week. Each week we would be allocated to either visit an elderly parishioner or to do odd jobs around the church. Christine, who was older than me and lived in our street, was also a member. She knew my family very well. One particular week we had both been chosen to dust around the altar and to vacuum the carpet. It was the first time I had done these tasks and I was nervous at the thought of just the two of us being in the church alone.

My apprehension stemmed from two incidents that happened at the church to my mother and me when we were attending Mass, which gave us the idea that the ghost may have been following us to church. Twice, when we were the only two people in the pew on the front row, a third, unseen person joined us. We both looked up at the same time to see who was making their way along the pew, jolting and rattling the seats as they moved towards us. Nobody was there, but we could see the impressions of footsteps moving across the soft knee rest as they walked over it. Then two imprints settled on it next to my mother as if someone was kneeling on it. This was very unnerving for us and was made worse by us having to stay where we were because we did not want to cause a disturbance in the middle of the service. We tested the knee rests time and time again to see if we could leave an indentation on them but they were quite new at the time and always sprung back into shape immediately.

Father O'Meara let us into the locked church through the presbytery door after helping us to find the vacuum cleaner and the dusters. His housekeeper was nowhere to be seen. It amused us to see him being so domesticated. He was a large, round-bellied man with a jolly disposition. In his younger days he had been a wrestler, which showed in his build. He knew both of us well, but he did not have much time to spèak to us at that moment, so he

Holy Rosary church.

The exterior of the church.

Above: Father O'Meara (on the left).

Left: The altar inside the church.

scurried off and left us to it. The altar and its red carpet were already spotless, but we went through the motions of cleaning it anyway. Father O'Meara came into the church after five minutes or so to see if we needed the lights switching on. It was a lovely church, clean, and brightly decorated. I suppose I could say it was quite modern for its day. We could see just fine, so he turned and left us once more, disappearing through a side door which led to back to his house. 'He startled me just then,' said Christine. I looked towards her to see her polishing the altar rails. 'Me too,' I said, as I untangled the flex of the cleaner from around my feet.

'I feel a bit scared in here. Do you?' asked Christine. I hadn't thought of it until she said it, but yes, I felt afraid also and I didn't know why – but before I could answer, two swing doors at the back of the church suddenly burst open, causing a violent crash as if some huge force had belted through them. The commotion echoed around the church, stopping us in our tracks. This was quickly followed by the sound of footsteps running down a centre aisle then into a pew. We stood motionless as we looked up the aisle to see the cause of the chaos. All we could see was a row of seats being jolted and the sound of footsteps scurrying in amongst them.

We dropped everything immediately and ran helter-skelter out of the church in search of Father O'Meara. We ran through the side door and along a corridor that led to the presbytery. He had heard us thundering along, falling up a small flight of steps in our haste. His stout figure appeared at the far end of the corridor. With his jaw slack and his eyes wide, he asked in bewilderment:

'Whatever is the matter?'

'Sss… something's just charged in through the swing doors at the back of the church, but… but all the outside doors are locked and we couldn't see anything!' we both stuttered together.

'Oh!' he said, and brushed past us as he immediately headed for the church. 'There couldn't be anyone in there beside yourselves, because you're the only ones I've let in.' He drew a big bunch of keys from his pocket and waved them at us. 'These never leave me,' he said, as he tried to reassure us. 'Come on – follow me!' he ordered. Nervously, we scurried behind him. As we entered the church, I tried to prevent the side door from closing on us because I wanted to make sure our escape route was easily accessible if needed, but it kept closing of its own accord. I quickly gave up and decided it would be safer to stick with Father O'Meara as he checked out the church.

When he had finished, we stood in front of the main altar and looked down the length of the church. Father O'Meara took out a small black pocketbook like a policeman's. He began to chuckle as he wrote something down. 'Did you know that the church is haunted?' he asked calmly. Before we could answer, he added, 'It was only the ghost you heard; it won't harm you.' His voice took on a more serious tone as he explained to us that we were not the only people to have come across it. He told us that a priest was once found dead inside a confessional box, and he thought perhaps it was his ghost, and that he wasn't one little bit afraid of it and said we should not be either. But to me, that story did not fit. Just because someone dies in a church, it does not automatically mean they will haunt it. I had seen a sweet little old lady die in the church one Sunday morning. It happened just as everyone was leaving their seats after Mass. She was only three feet or so from the swing doors when she just gently and gracefully slid to the floor and died on the spot. But I could not see it being her ghost either. This ghost was too noisy to be the priest or the old lady. But I did not dismiss his explanation that the church was haunted in its own right.

I felt slightly relieved, but I still had a small worry at the back of my mind that it might be 'our' ghost and did not like the idea of it trailing our footsteps like a pet dog.

Since Brideen had left home and joined the Army I had to sleep in our attic bedroom alone (except for when she was home on leave). The room was large and covered the whole of the attic floor. The staircase to it led directly into the middle of the room with a rail surrounding the opening. Part of the rail was boxed in and formed a table-like top, which we found to be very useful. Unfortunately, this room, even though it was cosy, was probably the most haunted room in the house; the front bedroom that Sandra and Edmond had once shared was also very affected. Many times, either through the day or night, footsteps could be heard moving about or their owner bumping into the furniture as they went by. Frequently, I was jolted in my bed as the 'thing' clumsily crashed into it as it leaned over me. I could feel its eyes boring straight into me. Inches away from my face, it blew out little puffs of air. It came so close that I was too terrified to move a fraction and wished my face were buried under the blankets. Even after it was gone, I could not look up, just in case it was still there, even though I would not see it in the dark room. If it was moving around somewhere else in the room, I felt braver and would deliberately make a noise as it usually stopped moving then. But more often than not, when things were quiet again, it would start once more on its clumsy walkabout.

Late one morning during an Easter break I was quietly sitting in my room writing a letter to Laura, as I often did. At this time she was living in Brussels with her husband, Alex, who was from Belgium. I had planned to write her a good long letter this time, and was comfortably perched on the edge of my bed. I was well into writing my third page when my deep thoughts were disturbed by the sound of footsteps coming from the far side of the room. I sat very still and listened. Moving just my eyes, and without lifting my head, I looked in the direction of the footsteps, which proceeded to move around erratically. I saw nothing there, but held my breath as 'it' came closer to me. It bumped into the dressing table, causing it to tilt slightly. Then it hit the foot of my bed. For some unknown reason that I cannot explain, I felt rather brave at that moment and found the courage to speak out, even though I knew a noise of any sort would stop it in its tracks.

'I know you're there!' I said with confidence. Just as I predicted it instantly stopped moving. I remained very still, breathing as quietly as I could, and waited. I didn't have to wait long, for only two minutes or so later it started to wander about again. I wanted to try and communicate with it. I was sure it could hear me just as plainly as I could hear it. I spoke again, little caring whether it stopped or not. 'I want to be your friend and help you. I know you can hear me. Don't be afraid.' Who was I trying to fool? I was the one afraid. I wasn't really brave at all, but I managed to keep my composure all the same, and came up with a plan.

The ballpoint pen I was using was very distinctive. It was bright orange and over large. It was the only pen in the house like it. Purposely I stood up and carefully placed it and a sheet of notepaper on my box-like table in the centre of the room. At the same time, I gave my new unseen pal instructions to write a message if it was unable to speak, or make a mark on the paper if it could not write. I kept my eye on the pen as I slowly inched my way towards the stairs. I was terrified that it just might start to write or do something before I left the room, even though that was what I wanted it to do. I lost my nerve. I quickly told it that I was going downstairs and would be back later. With my heart in my mouth, and my short-lived courage well and truly gone, I scuttled down the stairs.

My mother was in the kitchen. Without giving anything away, or telling her what I was up to, I quietly sat and ate lunch with her. I tried to behave normally. Although I was shaking inside, she did not seem to notice. An hour passed. Although nervous, I managed to leave the room calmly. I made my way up to my room, worrying as to what I might find. I wished now, as I sometimes did before, that I had a periscope so I could see into the room in advance. The moment I reached the top of the attic stairs my eyes went directly to the pen and paper. What an anti-climax! There was no profound message – instead, the sod had pinched my pen! Later, I finished my letter to Laura adding – 'I'm sorry for a change from blue ink to green but…'!

Some months after that incident, I was alone once more in the room playing Elvis Presley records. I was a big fan and danced around the room to the music as teenagers do. It was daytime but you would hardly have known, as it was so dark and rainy outside. The small window in the ceiling of the room did not allow much light in at the best of times, so I had the overhead light on. As I danced and swung my arms about I was facing towards the light switch, which was situated approximately six feet away from me at the top of the stairs. Something caught my eye which did not seem quite right: it was the shadow of my arm with my finger pointing at the chimney flue. It took only a split second for me to realise that it was not my shadow at all, because it remained on the wall after I moved my arm down! I gasped with shock. My skin began to crawl and I just wanted to get out of there. I was not very good at panicking or hysterics so I instead inched my way to the stairs. I was, all the same, completely terrified at the thought of having to pass close to the shadow to make my escape, but I had no choice, as the stairs were my only way out. The shadow was around four feet up the wall from the floor and only inches from the top of the stairs. Making myself as thin as I could, I edged my way past the image to the stairs and fled.

I bounded into the kitchen to find Mamma and her sister-in-law, Millie, sitting by the fire, chatting away. I didn't know we had a visitor until then. Aunt Millie looked across and smiled at me as I noisily appeared in the open doorway. She did not mind that I had not greeted her when I blurted out what I had just seen. I allowed Mamma and Aunt Millie to lead the way up to my room. By now the shadow had gone. I showed them where it had been and demonstrated what I'd been doing and where I was standing when it appeared. We found it impossible to throw a shadow on the wall where I saw it, unless we stood as close as four inches or so from the wall at the top of the stairs. I was horrified to realise that meant I did have to squeeze past the thing in order to get down the stairs.

I was really surprised to find how readily Aunt Millie accepted my story. She believed me without even batting an eyelid. I thought she would be like almost everyone else and think of ghosts as nonsense. We analysed and discussed the situation but could not find a satisfactory answer to explain the incident. It did, however, leave us wondering if the pointed finger was signifying something to do with the chimney flue.

It was difficult to know the past history of the house. All the information we could obtain was names of previous occupiers, which told us very little. On searching the archives it was found that the building of the house and eight others in the street was approved on 16 February 1877. A Mr Joseph Holmes owned them. There is a slight puzzle, however: the original plans of the houses show them to be different to the actual buildings – as if things had been changed after the plans had been drawn up. The plans show bay windows that were not on the houses in Grant Street but which were on the houses on the other side of Roundhay Road.

As far as we could establish, nothing had been built on the land before the house was constructed. The previous history of the area and also that of Glover Street was found to be mainly of military camps, garrisons and such like. So it can only be assumed that the ghosts probably originated from a previous occupier or occupiers of the house itself.

Our lives could not revolve around the ghosts, so we mostly pushed thoughts of them to the back of our minds. But it was not always so easy to forget them. It was difficult to avoid moving around the house without one's senses suddenly being aroused, telling you that something was very close by. A noise as soft as a whisper, a movement as gentle as a breath would be enough to raise the hair on one's head and make the blood run cold and cause a hasty retreat from a room.

The suggestion of leaving the house never arose because my father insisted that there was nothing wrong with it and accused my mother of fantasising about the ghosts. He got annoyed with her whenever she mentioned them. She'd then point out that he was always working away so he hardly lived in the house, so how would he know? In spite of my father's opinion, other people who came to visit, knowing nothing about the problems in the house, were also to experience strange things going on in it from time to time.

My mother's sister, Della, and her daughter, Helen, came over for a short stay from Ireland. As my father was away, Mamma gave them the use of her large double bedroom and she slept elsewhere. A small wardrobe had been emptied for their use. They decided to leave their unpacking on the first night until the morning, because they were too tired after their long journey. The next day they complained of sleeping very badly because they had been scared out of their wits in the dead of night by a peculiar noise coming from inside the wardrobe. As they lay in the bed trembling, neither of them could identify the sound that was disturbing them and they had no idea what was causing it. Even though the noise kept them awake for quite some time, they were too afraid get out of the bed to investigate it, and waited until the light of morning before daring to open the wardrobe door. They were surprised to find it empty except for a wooden toy train on the shelf. (It was a gift that my mother had bought for them to take back to a child in Ireland.) By moving the train quickly back and forth along the shelf they produced the same noise that they had both heard during the night. Needless to say, their visit was a short one.

Four

THE GHOSTS

One warm, sunny morning of 1962, Mamma and I were in the kitchen. We were the only two people in the house. No thoughts of the ghosts had entered my mind for some time because nothing of any significance had happened recently to remind me of them. But they had a way of catching me by surprise, making themselves known just when I least expected them.

I went off to the newsagents around the corner to buy my favourite 'pop' magazine. When I returned a few minutes later, my mother was still in the kitchen busily sorting out the washing. I decided to get out of her way and went upstairs to read my magazine.

The window of my parents' bedroom was thrown wide open to the world, and sunshine was pouring in. Warm gentle air billowed out the curtains as it pushed through them. The room looked so bright and wonderfully inviting. I chose to read in here rather than my own room. I left all the doors open to allow air to circulate around the house. I threw myself upon the double bed and made myself comfortable. I didn't get any further than glancing at the front cover of my magazine when the door at the foot of the stairs slammed shut. I assumed that Mamma had closed it as she went by. At the moment of impact, the sound of a small child bursting into sobs rose up the stairs, giving me the impression that the door had been shut in its face when it was about to go through it. I was baffled as to who the child could be. There was no one on the stairs a few moments ago when I came up them. And as far as I knew, no one else was in the house except me and my mother. I came to the conclusion that it had to be Amanda, even though I had not seen her for quite some time. I called out her name, even though I was still puzzled as to why I had not noticed her when I returned from the shop (and why Mamma said nothing about her being in the house).

The crying became louder as she moved up the stairs, combined with the sound of the toes of little shoes, stubbing against each step as she climbed them. 'Amanda, come to Auntie Colette.' I called again. 'Poor baby, has someone trapped you on the stairs?' There was no reply other than heavy sobs, probably the saddest I've ever heard. At that moment, it crossed my mind that perhaps it was not Amanda, but some other child unknown to me. I could see the top of the stairs through the open door. I waited for Amanda or some other child to come into sight, but she was taking such a long time to reach the top of the stairs that I got off the bed and went to fetch her. I crossed the room and the moment I reached the door, the crying stopped. My eyes searched down the staircase, but all I could see was the stairs. There was no child there at all.

I stood perplexed, my mind unable to comprehend what was going on. I wanted to run to safety, but was too afraid to do so just in case I stood on it, or had to pass through it. 'Mam, Mam!' I called out repeatedly to my mother until she opened the door at the foot of the stairs.

'What is it?' she answered at last, with a tinge of annoyance in her voice. The normality of her standing there holding the door ajar produced a strange contrast against the abnormality of the situation. I did not speak, but watched her face change from a frown to bewilderment as I moved sidelong, at high speed, down the stairs towards her, trying desperately not to put my feet down as I descended (which proved impossible). From that time on, I always inspected the stairs before I used them.

That same year, I was startled out of my sleep when a heavy blow hit me across my stomach. It happened so quickly; I had no time to think about it. I did not even open my eyes, but as my attic bedroom was so dark anyway, I could not have been able to see a thing. My instant reaction was to sit bolt upright and pat the bedding in front of me. I instantly felt a small arm with its hand and fingers resting across my legs. I moved my hands back along the arm to find its owner, but there was nothing more to feel – and the arm was gone.

I could usually feel the presence of a ghost as I walked into a room. The first indication I felt of one being there was a creeping sensation that ran along my scalp as my hair desperately tried to stand on end. Only the weight and length of the hairs prevented it from doing so. The closer the ghost, the more my body responded. The fine hairs on my arms joined in, and these did manage to stand completely upright. The sensation would then run down my back and legs. The feeling can be described as being similar to the body's reaction to cold.

I seemed to be little more sensitive than anyone else around in feeling the presence of a ghost. Whenever Mamma retired to bed for the night, she asked me to give her bedroom the 'all clear' first. After this, she went to bed happily. If something did happen to be lurking in her room, we madly scrambled out of it with our hearts beating wildly. Then Mamma slept elsewhere.

As well as members of the family, the ghosts began to attack visitors and friends who came to the house. Gail and I had become firm friends almost from the time when I first moved to Grant Place. There was only three months' difference in our ages, she being the elder. She lived a few streets away, and spent much of her time at our house. She often stayed overnight, sleeping in Brideen's bed when she was away in the Army. Gail sometimes spent more time at our house than her own. This was fine by my family and especially me, as I didn't have to sleep in the room alone.

We came to the conclusion that one of the ghosts in the house liked to tease Gail because it often hit her on the head as she climbed the attic stairs to my room. We had the impression that the ghost would beat down on her head by leaning over the bannister from the room above. One of these incidents I found to be amusing, although she did not think so.

My friend Gail.

It was when we galloped up the stairs as usual, with Gail leading. She abruptly stopped in her stride and gave a little cry. I almost ran into the back of her. I looked up to see her head repeatedly jerk forward as if she was again being hit by something. I could hear the thuds landing on her head. I received one blow also. But this time, it must have hit Gail once too often, because she lost her temper with it. 'I'm sick of you!' she screamed. Her arms flailed in all directions as she punched the air and fought her way up the stairs. 'Let me hit you,' she yelled in frustration, unable to see her assailant and land a punch. 'I'll kill you! I'll kill you!' As she reached the room her eyes swiftly darted back and forth to scour every corner, with her fist held high, ready for any conflict. But there was nothing there for her to hit. She made it clear from her scowl that she was not very pleased with me either, because all I could do was laugh at the irony of her statement. Remarkably, though, it eased up from hitting her after that.

Alas, that was not the end of her encounters with the ghosts, for not long after, she saw a man dressed in a striped suit standing in the corner of my room. He was laughing at her. Although I was in the room at the time, I did not see him. One moment she was chatting happily and the next, she was screaming hysterically. I turned to see where she was pointing at the far corner of the room but I saw nothing.

By 1963, Brideen had left home for good and had met her future husband, Deitor, who was also in the Army. Gail and I both worked at the C.W.S. shoe manufacturers. Her family had moved to another area, which made it difficult for her to get to work, so for a while she moved into our house and shared my room. Now that we were aged sixteen and fully trained, we earned good wages, and decided to have a clean sweep and replace all our old clothes with new. We completely emptied my wardrobe, which we were to share.

As our new clothes accumulated, Gail's new dresses were neatly hung in the left-hand side of the wardrobe and mine to the right, with our new coats hanging between them in the centre. To my disappointment, one of my lovely new dresses shrunk after the first wash and the shop would not change it. But all was not lost, because my cousin Freddie Walters and his wife Betty had recently moved into the house next door and she was considering buying the dress from me, as it was now just her size.

A week later, in a haze of perfume and dolled up to the eyes, Gail and I put on our coats, turned off the bedroom light and dashed downstairs. We were going to a posh works do, and it was getting late. Mam, Dad, Conrad and Gary were in the kitchen. We quickly said our goodbyes to them and opened the back door to leave. At that very moment, Betty was standing on the doorstep with her hand poised in readiness to knock before walking in.

'Oh! Colette. I'm glad I caught you before you left.'

I stepped aside to let her enter.

'Freddie wants to take me out tonight; we've been invited to an engagement party. I'll have that dress if you still have it,' she said hopefully.

'Err… yes. I do still have it. I'll go and fetch it.' Her timing was faultless for her, but not for me. I quickly turned on my heel and dashed back up the two flights of stairs, turning on the lights as I went. I knew exactly where the dress was hanging in the wardrobe because I purposely left it in front of the others with the idea that Betty might be around for it. And only two minutes or so ago, when Gail and I removed our coats from the wardrobe, the dress was the last thing I saw before closing the door.

The instant I switched on the bedroom light I noticed that the wardrobe door was wide open and all my dresses had been pushed right over to the left, in amongst Gail's clothes, leaving my side of the wardrobe empty. I tugged at the dresses to slide them back, but they seemed to be caught up somehow and pulled tightly together. I patted about to feel for the obstruction and my hand came to rest on something soft but solid in amongst the clothes. It moved slightly when I prodded it and I could not imagine what it might be. After a failed attempt to dislodge it by pushing and shoving, I managed to part the dresses and look between them – and I gasped so hard in horror at what I saw that I almost swallowed my tongue as I unintentionally sucked it to the back of my throat. My hands had been resting on the shoulder of a man in a green-striped jacket as he crouched amongst the dresses. He was rocking slightly on his haunches. As I moved my hands away, a sickening shock of disbelief swept over me which no words can describe. Moving like a zombie, I slowly backed away. I switched off the light and went down the stairs. I had little recollection of taking the dress from the wardrobe as I was too numbed. Without a word, I handed the dress to Betty and left the house.

Gail was just as aware of the haunting in the house as I was, but for a reason I cannot explain, I found it impossible to tell her what I'd just seen. How could I expect her to believe me when I could hardly believe it myself? My evening was ruined. I was in a state of shock. All I could see in my mind's eye was the green herringbone weave on the shoulder of the man's jacket, and my hands resting on it.

Later, when we returned home, I went straight up to the bedroom. I needed to check that I had not mistaken something else for a man. The wardrobe door was still open and I looked inside. Other than my dresses being a little disarranged, there was nothing else amiss.

A posh works do. This was the same evening as the episode with the wardrobe. From left to right: Two friends, myself and Gail.

I could clearly see that there was nothing in the wardrobe other than clothes. It even looked rather bare. I looked through the clothes, felt around them, but could not find anything remotely like a green jacket, let alone a man. I never spoke of this to anyone and pushed the incident to the back of my mind for many years.

Shortly after that incident, Gail and I were in my room doing our hair for another night out. At the age of seventeen this was a very serious business. It being the sixties, the bouffant was the trend, which required some skill and effort to get right. With a lot of practice, we both managed it very well. I used the dressing-table mirror to do my hair and Gail stood beside me using the wardrobe mirror to do hers. We shared the same hairbrush. Silently, we worked methodically through our hair for five minutes or so, in turn, picking up the brush and placing it back on the edge of the dressing table for easy reach. We were so well practised at this that it was almost a ritual. Gail leaned across me and patted the top of the dressing table without taking her eyes away from the mirror. Her other hand, still on her head, clutched at a clump of hair.

'Where's the brush?' she asked.

'It should be on the dressing table.'

'It isn't.'

'But I've just put it there. It must have fallen down.'

'I can't see it anywhere,' Gail whined. 'It's not there!'

This was a bother; it just had to be around somewhere. We were both stuck with our hair only half done: we had to find it, but it was nowhere to be seen. We spent the next fifteen minutes searching every possible and impossible place for it, but to no avail. We just could not fathom out where the brush had gone. We knew that neither of us had moved an inch away from the spot. But the brush simply disappeared from underneath our noses and we had not seen or heard anything to account for it. The hairbrush was never to be found.

The hairbrush incident wasn't frightening, just very annoying as well as mystifying and bore no comparison at all to the most terrifying ordeal that we both suffered later, which I found to be the most difficult to cope with.

It was ten o'clock in the evening when we went to bed. We had retired early because we had to be up in time to start work at seven thirty the following morning. Gail, as usual, had the job of turning off the light because the switch was on the wall nearest to her bed. A few moments after we had quietly settled down to sleep, the overhead light switched back on. The sudden glare caused me to screw up my eyes, but before I could open them, the light was switched back off again. I simply thought Gail must have done it and vaguely wondered why I hadn't heard her get out of bed. The room was completely silent.

Seconds later, I heard her moaning and groaning from her bed. Because the room was always as black as pitch at night unless the moon was shining in, I could not see anything. I opened my mouth to speak to her but was distracted when the blankets at the foot of my bed were tugged at. A moment or so later, the small tugs became a big yank which lifted my blankets up high. The cold air rushed onto my feet and legs followed by what I can only describe as a dog's tail rapidly wagging across my shins. We no longer had a dog by then; Victor had long since gone, having been taken on by a farmer. Then, adding horror to horror, a pair of thin, long-fingered hands placed themselves on my stomach and proceeded to inch their way up my body. They crawled underneath my own hands, which were resting on my chest. I gripped the bony fingers to push them away, but I couldn't, I was not strong enough. As they neared my throat, I thought I was about to die. My mouth had opened but I only produced a silent scream. My hair convulsed along my scalp. And all the while, I could hear Gail moaning.

My life or my sanity was saved by Gail's moans when they erupted into the shrillest of screams and caused the horrid atmosphere in the darkness to crack in two. She leapt from her bed and switched on the light. At the same time, my hands sank to my chest as the 'others' dissolved from under them. 'Col… Colette!' Gail screamed hysterically. 'Something held me down on the bed and I couldn't move – then the light came on. Then went off.' She began to cry. I could not speak or blink. I simply lay there, stupefied. I looked across at her, unable to bring my senses together. After a while, we both fled downstairs to my mother. When she saw us tear into the living room her face drained white. She knew something was wrong by the way we looked. She was about to go to bed, but now she was just as frightened as we were.

The three of us were too afraid to sleep alone and Gail would not go back into my room, so we all shared my mother and father's big double bed. (Fortunately my father was away at the time.) But it didn't do much good, because long into the night we screamed and cowered because the 'thing' made repeated attempts to come at me again: only by kicking and screaming at it did I keep it at bay. As far as I was concerned, I had encountered a demon from hell that night.

The next day, Mam went to see Father O'Meara and told him the whole story. She asked him if he would come and bless the house. He did listen, but refrained from a visit, and instead instructed her to sprinkle holy water in every room. She collected about a gallon of holy water; the house was going to get more than a sprinkle. Gail and I slept with my mother for the following three nights as we were still very frightened. We didn't sleep in my room for another month.

It was following that dreadful incident that Mam decided to bring in an exorcist. Until that time I thought these people were fictional. Mam felt she had no choice, as my father would not hear of us leaving the house because he couldn't see any reason for it, so she did not tell him. She knew that he'd be angry if she told him what she was doing, and that he'd say she was mad. If she was mad, then we all must be mad.

The exorcist was a priest. He told my mother that he could feel evil in the house. I had to agree with him there: so could I. Also, he said there was something else more sinister than ghosts. He told her that there are some villages in Africa where the evil is so bad that a priest such as himself found it very difficult to enter, making it almost impossible to perform an exorcism. But he assured Mamma that he could do one in our house.

It wasn't dramatic as one might expect; he didn't do any more than say a few prayers and splash holy water about. Mam was a little dismayed when he didn't even move out of the kitchen. He just gave her some holy water to sprinkle around the bedrooms, which she did almost every day anyway. It was over in minutes. Needless to say, it did not work – if anything, it probably made matters worse.

The mention of Africa must have got Mamma's mind working overtime. She amused and amazed us by finding a witch doctor – in Leeds! He offered to rid the house of the spirits. He was the last person we would have expected to have around. With tongue-in-cheek, she accepted his kind offer. The witch doctor was not dressed in a bizarre fashion as one might expect from what we see on films and television: he wore an ordinary suit. He wasn't one bit like a witch doctor. He was a very pleasant middle-aged West-Indian gentleman. Alas, his attempts to exorcise the house also failed; on entering the house, he was terrified and complained that an evil presence was overwhelming him, making him too afraid to face it. He scarpered. No further attempts were ever made to exorcise the house.

Years went by before I dared to speak of that night for fear that it might reoccur. I did not know for all that time that speaking about it made no difference. Thank God, that terrifying experience was never to take place again.

We didn't always discuss the ghostly incidents with each other. We mostly tried to make sense of our strange experiences by ourselves the best way we could. It was difficult to talk about them to anyone, especially when we knew we were not likely to be believed. Having to convince oneself that one was not crazy was enough for a start. But occasionally things did spill out. I can still see the fear in Conrad's eyes as he confided in me one day and told me what had just happened to him:

I was sitting on the edge of my bed, inspecting the contents of my pocket, and I looked up to see the figure of a man standing in the open doorway. He had a small beard and was wearing strange clothes, not unlike the type worn in Charles Dickens' days. The man was peering at the door that opened onto the attic stairs – as if he was waiting for something. Slowly, he turned around and lined up a pair of sinister eyes with mine. I was too frightened to move;

I had no choice but to remain still. The horrid little man continued to hold his loathsome stare until I somehow summoned up enough courage to call for help. Only then did the disturbing figure disperse.

Another time, when Conrad was around twelve years old, he said:

I was going up the stairs carrying a comic close to my chest. Something brushed past me when I was halfway up. As soon as I reached the landing, I realized that the comic was gone. I re-traced my steps, thinking that I must have dropped it, but it was nowhere to be found. Although I knew full well that I was the only one on the stairs my logic told me that someone must have sneaked it away from me as a prank. Eventually, I had to admit to myself that this was impossible. The comic turned up two weeks later, under my pillow.

The well-lit, almost bare rooms of the cellar seemed to be innocuous. They were mainly used for storing coal and vegetables. Mamma kept the cellars tidy, so it was easy to know where everything was. In one of the rooms were Dad's large wooden toolbox, a few tins of paint, and an old chair. Sitting on the chair, as it did for many years, was a three-foot tall Guy Fawkes. I suppose it was unusual to have a Guy in one's cellar as tradition has it that the effigy be burnt on the top of a bonfire on 5 November, but we were never able to bring ourselves to destroy it because this one had not been crudely made like most of them were, but very well put together by Mamma. She was clever with her hands, and wonderful at involving herself in our childhood games. She had made the Guy for Alfred and Edmond when they were still boys. I often played with it as a child and treated it like a doll. So it held happy memories for us, thus its place on the chair.

For most of the time in the early years of our living in Grant Street, there were no reports of anything strange happening in the cellars. Unfortunately, as time went by, things were to change and the cellars began to develop a frighteningly eerie feel to them. Noises were heard, such as a scurrying across the floors as we walked down the steps. The sounds were much too loud to be a mouse or any other small creature. We found objects had been moved to different places to where we had left them.

Mamma had been puzzled for three days or so because each time she went into the cellar, she found the Guy sitting on the toolbox instead of the chair. Each time she returned it to the chair. She did not speak of this until she had eliminated the chances that someone in the family may have moved it, although for the life of her she could not think why they should. She only spoke up after I told her that I heard something running across the cellar floor as I went down the steps. And on reaching the bottom, I saw the chair with the Guy sitting on it, rocking back and forth. I only saw this because I always rushed down the steps at high speed, hoping to catch out whatever was making the scurrying noises. I wasn't brave; my fast descents to the cellars were usually only for self-preservation. I would hastily snatch up the item I'd gone to fetch, usually a vegetable or a shovel of coal, then make my escape back up the steps with the same swiftness as a rabbit being chased by a fox. I could not help but do this because I usually felt a sensation that something was running behind me, trying to grab at my back. I would arch it as I fled, gasping in fear.

Five

TONY

B y the time I reached the age of eighteen Glover Street and the whole area had been flattened to make way for a flyover and new houses. It saddened me to know that I would never again see the house where I was born, which I considered to be my true home. The place that held all my best childhood memories was no more. A wilderness of rubble was my only souvenir. Even St Matthew's, now the only building still standing, was earmarked for demolition. The steeple by now had become unsafe. The church still looked big, black and ugly, but I knew I was going to miss it. This was perhaps the first time in living memory that one was able to see the rolling hills of the landscape since before this area of Leeds was built up. I could almost visualise how the area must have looked in the days long ago when General Elliot had his camp on this very site in 1766.

By now, Brideen had married Deitor, a serving soldier, and left the Army. Then Deitor was transferred to Malta for two years. During this time, I met Tony, my future husband. He was twenty-two. I'd never dreamed for a moment that I was going to be his girlfriend, let alone his wife one day. We did not hit it off on the first, second or third occasion that we met. Our getting together was a rather slow, unplanned process and nowhere near as romantic as my parents' or grandparents' meeting.

It was all through a crush that Gail had on a friend of Tony's. Every time we saw Brian he seemed to be with Tony. I always succumbed to her wish and melted into the background while she chatted to Brian.

In the 1960s Gail and I often visited the Fford Grene pub, it being the liveliest local in our area. Sometimes things got a little out of hand in there and the occasional punch up was not unknown. But that did not interfere with the popularity of the pub. The clientele were of mixed ages, races, and background who all enjoyed the music and atmosphere that live rock bands created. The bands helped to draw the crowds, who never hesitated to boo them off the stage if they came below standard. This is where I spoke to Tony for the first time.

'Oh! Colette, Colette – Brian's there!' Gail squealed excitedly as she spotted him across the room.

'Great!' I said. I had to chuckle at her reactions whenever she saw him. She behaved just like a young schoolgirl; you would never think she was eighteen. Brian was fair, tall and good-looking. He was a really nice person and I understood why she liked him. I automatically expected things to run smoothly for her with Brian as neither of us ever had trouble in attracting the opposite sex. I watched her as she pushed a path through the throng of people heading towards Brian. Her cheerful cheek amused me, and I watched with interest for Brian's reaction. I could not hear her speak when she reached him, but I detected a genuine smile from Brian, that indicated to me that all was fine between them. A few moments later Tony stood next to me with a pint of beer in his hand. I wasn't sure if he'd made this move on purpose to speak to me, or if he was just trying to get a closer look at the stage.

'It's a good band tonight, isn't it?' I said, testing his motive.

'No! It's a load of crap!'

His abruptness took me by surprise. I felt offended and annoyed with myself for speaking to him. I turned away from him and spoke no more. He made no attempt to speak to me either.

The second time I spoke to Tony was weeks later when I only uttered the words 'thank you' after he gave me and my friends a lift home in his new Mini. The third time was again due to a lift home from a coffee bar in town. It was sheer coincidence that Brian and Tony happened to walk in while Gail and I were there. Gail, of course, made her usual beeline for Brian. It was the perfect chance for her to finally hook him. I remained sitting with some friends. When it was time to leave, Tony offered Brian, Gail and me a lift home. I refused. 'Please, Colette do it for me,' pleaded Gail. She knew full well that it would mean that I would be paired up with Tony and I did not want that. Not after the way he spoke to me at the Ffordy. But she was my friend and things were looking very promising for her with Brian. Reluctantly, I gave in.

We left and Tony walked beside me and found my discontent very amusing.

'Mind your face doesn't crack,' he said, trying to make light of my annoyance with him.

'What do you mean? I asked, pretending not to understand.

'Well, if you smile your face might crack,' he chuckled.

It was the first time I'd heard that expression and I could not help but give a small smile. His jollity began to soften me, and I walked less reluctantly to the car. It wasn't the best chat-up line that I'd ever heard, but it somehow worked and he slowly grew on me. I thought he was tall enough at 5ft 10in or so. He had nice hazel eyes and very dark hair and kind of resembled my brother Edmond, which wasn't a bad thing as Edmond was very handsome. So I guessed he must have looked okay.

Tony, being a steady, good-humoured and reliable type, hit it off right away with my parents and the rest of my family. My mother detected a refined manner in him that she especially liked. My father was impressed by his conscientiousness towards his work as a pattern weaver. So, as far as they were concerned, I was onto a winner with him. It did not matter to them that he was not rich or fancy because that sort of thing did not impress them, as they were not materialistic; it was the person that counted with them.

The last thing I wanted to do was to tell Tony about the ghosts because I had learned to keep my mouth firmly shut. I knew he, like most people, would find the supernatural hard to believe in, simply because of their lack of experience with ghosts. However, I could not prevent Mamma, in spite of me asking her not to, telling Tony all about the house and its problems. He surprised me when he did not scoff as I expected him to, but instead stated that he'd always held an open mind on the subject of ghosts.

That made me feel more relaxed about the situation, but it still didn't loosen my tongue very much, and Tony never pressed me to speak about it. A few months after I met Tony, Gail and her family moved away from Leeds and went to live in Tadcaster. She finished with Brian after a short engagement. It was just not to be. I saw very little of her thereafter, but we still kept in touch by sending Christmas cards and the occasional letter.

Tony and I decided to get married. In the weeks leading up to our wedding on 26 March 1966, I saw a great bargain of a king-size bed in a sale. We were not looking to buy a bed just yet, but at only £40 it would have been foolish of us to let it go. We were only going to have to buy one later anyway. So we bought it. The only problem was what do we do with it in the meantime; I quickly decided that I wanted to use it, and that was that.

The bed was duly delivered, but we were unable to get it up the narrow attic stairwell to my bedroom. I was very disappointed, as it was a lovely bed and I really wanted to sleep in it. To solve the problem, it was decided that I would have to move into the front bedroom on the floor below where it would fit. That idea was fine by me. It was a nice big sunny room. It had not been in use since Edmond and Sandra had moved out and went to live in their new home.

The bed was positioned and I started the task of making it up. I had not even finished it when I heard a noise coming from inside a cupboard. The last things on my mind at this time were the ghosts. I was too busy thinking about our wedding plans and our future. I stopped what I was doing and listened. I could hear the noise very clearly but I could not figure out what it could be. I bent down and opened the cupboard door. The instant I pulled on the knob, the noise ceased. Inside, I found boxes of games and jigsaw puzzles neatly stacked together. I had not seen them for quite some time and had forgotten about them. I guessed Mamma must have stored them there. I shook the boxes one by one in an attempt to trace the source of the noise. I opened a box of draughts and moved the pieces around with my fingers. Immediately on doing this I was able to identify the sounds I'd heard. This shocked me, because the pieces were placed snugly in the box and I had to finger them quite roughly to reproduce the noise exactly. I quickly put everything back as it was and shut the door. Even before I backed away, the noise started up again and startled me. Hearing it for the second time served to confirm that the noise did in fact come from the draughts. Thereafter, I frequently heard the items in the cupboard being played with but I could never find anything to account for it. There was also another incident involving the same cupboard.

The dressing table in the room was against the wall facing the foot of the bed. I used the bed as a seat to sit in front of it. One afternoon, I was sitting there putting rollers in my hair when I heard wallpaper rip. The sound came from the cupboard area, which was behind me to the right. I turned but could not see anything amiss. I scoured the walls of the whole room for torn wallpaper and saw that it was all intact. I stopped and remained still for a few seconds, but I didn't hear it again. I finished with my hair and went downstairs.

I casually mentioned the incident to my mother, who was just about to slip out of the house to see Betty, next door. She made no reply and just idly swept her gaze over me as I spoke. I took it that she wasn't really listening and thought no more about it.

A few minutes later, she returned with Betty. Following in their footsteps was another neighbour, who was also called Betty. We differentiated between the two women by calling them English Betty and Irish Betty. Irish Betty was my cousin's wife next door. English Betty lived next door to them.

Mamma had been listening to me after all and she told the two women about the wallpaper. She'd asked Irish Betty if the tearing sound could have come from her house on the off chance that I'd heard something from there. The answer was no. Irish Betty had been sitting downstairs in her kitchen with English Betty having a cup of tea. Betty checked her bedrooms and everything was fine, but for some reason the incident really intrigued them both. I could not really understand why this was, because very little had happened and I was sure there must have been a simple explanation for it. However, the four of us all went upstairs to my room to try and solve the mystery. Of course they couldn't see anything wrong with the wallpaper either.

Because the ripping sound had come from the cupboard area, we decided to pull it away from the wall. It was such a close fit to the wall we were unable to see behind it and could barely get our fingers around the back for leverage. The cupboard was very heavy and it took the strength of all of us to shift it.

We were astounded when we pulled it away to find that the wallpaper had not only been ripped but also torn upwards from the skirting board – an inconceivable situation. Speechless, we all watched mesmerised as a fine white power gently fell from behind the paper and settled on the floor to resemble a miniature pyramid. We all knew that it was impossible for anything, even a creature as small as a mouse, to fit behind that cupboard, let alone find room to rip the paper.

The situation was bad in my new room. It wasn't any better than my old room for creepy, scary things going on. And the ghost or ghosts were definitely noisier in here. One night I was dragged out of my sleep by a racket going on in the bedroom. Something was violently rapping the dressing-table handles on the drawers. On waking I automatically stretched out my legs as I moved to sit up. I quickly changed my mind about sitting up when the soles of my feet pressed against something very hard and weighty sitting on the foot of my bed. I froze to the spot. I was too afraid even to withdraw my feet so I left them pressing against 'it', and hoped that 'it' wouldn't notice them.

The handles on the dressing table resembled small doorknockers. Unlike real doorknockers, they did not hang loosely and were partly encased. Even with great deliberation, I found it impossible to flick them all at once as this 'thing' was doing. I was afraid to make the slightest move or even to take the smallest peek to see what was there. The reality of it was I did not want to see what was there because I was too terrified. The din continued for ten minutes or so, which to me felt like an eternity. Very slowly, the noise subsided. At the same time, the lump dissolved at my feet. Only now did I dare to move my toes slightly to feel around for it before deciding that it had gone. Even when the room returned to silence, I could not muster up enough courage to call out for help, for fear of 'it' still being around. Other than my toes, I did not move an inch until morning.

Another night, I was again rudely awakened by a frenzied commotion tearing around the room. It sounded like a battleground because furniture was being battered and banged about. Doors and drawers were violently wrenched open, only to be wildly slammed shut again.

My bed was rammed so hard I almost toppled out of it. Sitting bolt upright, I scanned the room to find the cause of the chaos. With the help of a street lamp outside, I could see quite well in the semi-darkness, unlike in the attic bedroom. To the left of my bed on the window side of the room was my grandfather's old tin trunk, dated from before the First World War when he was first in the Army. It was now in use as a blanket box. I could plainly see the silhouette of a man leaning over the trunk. He was frantically searching through it. He was slim and not very tall. He had a goatee beard, and was wearing a hat. I called out to him, but he was so intent on his frantic search that he did not heed me. I called out again, but this time he vanished without looking up, leaving the room silent – except for the sound of my gasps.

Six

HOMELESS

Tony and I married in March 1966. We bought a small house in the Potternewton area of Leeds. It was only a mile or so from Grant Place. The shoe factory where I worked closed down a few short months after our wedding. The shoe trade was suffering badly due to the imports of Italian shoes. A variety of short-term jobs followed until the spring of 1967. I was then in between jobs.

I was not used to being at home all day. Tony was out at work and I was alone. The house was too quiet. I'd done my chores already, and it was only eleven-thirty. My elderly next-door neighbours hadn't made a sound all morning, so I assumed they were out. I hadn't even seen a soul pass by in the street. I felt as if I was the only person left in the world. 'Where is everyone?' I asked myself. 'Have they left the planet?' Although it was spring, it was one of those windless, almost no weather days, being neither warm nor cold, and grey without rain. I decided to take a walk to my mother's house and visit a while. When I arrived, she was out. This brought about a slight twinge of loneliness which I'd never experienced before.

I let myself in, then made a pot of tea and waited for her to return. I expected her to be home for lunch and by now it was almost noon. I sat at the kitchen table where all life seemed to stem from in this house. I poured out a steaming mug of tea, and settled down to read yesterday's *Daily Mirror*.

Around ten minutes later my heart gave a little flip when I unexpectedly felt something silky and cold slowly wrap around my ankles and pass between my feet. My first thought was that it was a cat and it must have come up from the cellar. I glanced across to the cellar door but it was closed. I shuddered. I hadn't heard a sound. I sat motionless for a few moments before daring to lift the edge of the tablecloth to peer down at my feet. I fully expected to see a cat snuggling up to me. But there was no cat or anything else that I could see – yet I could still feel the movement brushing against my legs. Instantly, I knew that this must be the experience that Mamma had told us about. She often said she encountered something moving around her legs whilst in the kitchen. It was the first time that I had felt it. I was stunned but, for some reason, not terribly afraid. However, given my past experiences,

I leapt from the chair, trying to be careful as to where I placed my feet. I did not want to stand on it. When Mamma returned home, she found me sitting on the doorstep. I made some feeble excuse for being there.

Conrad and Mamma told me that since I left, the house was getting worse because the ghosts seemed to be getting more active. Conrad at the time was serving his apprenticeship as an auto-electrician, and worked in Sheepscar, which wasn't very far away. Recently, he said to me:

> Sometimes I came home at lunchtime but was too afraid to stay in the house alone if Mam was out, because regularly when I walked into the house I'd feel something there, lurking. In the silence of the house my senses were somehow more acute and I knew I was being watched. I could feel it. Sometimes I thought Mamma was in the house when I arrived home because I could hear the floors upstairs being swept. The first time I heard this, I called out to her. There was no answer so I went upstairs to find her.
>
> Sweep, sweep… sweep, sweep. The brushing sound continued to move from room to room and I followed it, but couldn't catch it up no matter how I tried.
>
> 'Mam! Mam! Where are you?' I called out repeatedly. She still didn't answer and was nowhere to be found because she wasn't there – nobody was there. I was alone in the house.

My mind went back to the previous November when we had at long last put the Guy Fawkes on a neighbour's bonfire. We'd all become jittery and frightened of it. It never collected dust, even after many years of sitting in the cellar. So a joint decision was made to burn it, just like the fate of any other Guy Fawkes on 5 November. Afterwards, I wished I had not done it. Deep down, I really wanted to keep him, even though he was an ugly little fellow. But I did wonder if things had become unsettled because of that action and made things worse, because I felt as if something had latched on to it.

In the early morning of 14 August 1967, things changed when my family's world was turned upside down. Tony and I were still asleep when someone began knocking on the door. It was a little after seven o'clock and time for Tony to get up for work. I leapt out of bed and went to the window. I pulled back the curtain and looked out to see who our visitor was. Down below I saw Conrad standing in the rain at the front door. He looked up as I tapped on the window to let him know that he had been heard. My immediate reaction was to worry. I wondered what on earth had brought him here at this time. It wasn't usual for him to call upon us like this.

I quickly put on my dressing gown and hurried down the stairs. I opened the door to the grey drizzly morning and shivered as Conrad walked in, accompanied by a rush of cold air. I noticed then that he was dressed in his good suit. He didn't speak but gave me a small smile as he passed me and walked into the living room.

'What are you doing here?' I called out over my shoulder as I closed the door and followed him.

'You'll have to come down to the house, Colette. Something's happened,' he said simply.

'Why, is something wrong?' I felt a knot tighten in my stomach.

'A wall has fallen down!'

'A wall?'

My half-asleep mind conjured up that he meant the backyard wall. It was the only one I could think of. It was tallish, and I supposed it could cause a problem of some sort if it were to fall down.

'But why have you come at this time to tell us that? Has someone been hurt?'

'No,' he answered calmly. 'Just come!'

Just then Tony appeared in the open doorway. He was already almost dressed. Then asked in surprise, 'What's up? Why are you wearing your suit at this time, Conrad?'

'I was wearing it last night. It was the first at hand this morning; I didn't have time to start sorting out clothes.' His answer was uncomfortable and the smile had dropped from his face.

'Something's happened down at the house,' I informed Tony. 'A wall's fallen down. Nobody's hurt.'

Conrad would not answer any more of our questions and gave nothing away by the expression on his face. He left us playing guessing games while I hastily washed and dressed and Tony made us all a quick breakfast before getting himself ready for work. A short time later, Conrad and I set off in his van, leaving Tony behind with his questions unanswered.

As we neared Grant Place a few minutes later, Conrad made an unexpected turn down the street before it and parked up.

'Why are you stopping here?' I asked.

'You will see,' he said, still keeping up the mystery.

We got out of the van and walked around the corner into Grant Place. I was astonished to see crowds of people standing all over the cobbled street. Fire engines, cars, and police cars lined the kerbs. But I couldn't see anything to account for it all.

'Come on now, Conrad; tell me what's going on,' I demanded.

'The house has fallen down,' he answered quietly.

I was now getting more exasperated with his game and found my temper beginning to rise. 'Don't be stupid,' I snapped. I could see that the house was still standing. Everything about it looked normal to me from where I stood at the top of the street, but I was somewhat surprised to see the yard wall still intact. I had pictured in my mind that the bricks were all over the footpath in the street. 'Come and look around the front,' said Conrad. I obeyed him immediately, and followed in his footsteps. The rain by now had turned into an odd spit here and there. It wasn't cold, but I shivered all the same as we turned into Grant Street.

A smaller crowd was gathered in the middle of the road opposite the house. The first thing that struck me about them was the way the people were all chatting to each other as if they were at a garden party. I looked away from them and gave my attention to the house. I was flabbergasted to see the whole frontage bulging outward in the shape of a big ugly boil, just waiting to burst. We walked down the street to get a closer look. One or two people, who, I assumed, recognised us, whispered to each other as we approached. On nearing the house, I could see the reason for the grotesque bulge. Lying sideways, across the inside of the front-room window, was the ceiling of the bedroom above. Looking up through the bedroom window, daylight could be seen through a gaping hole in the bedroom ceiling, caused by the huge chimneystack as it fell inwards. It was a strange sight. To see the curtains, still hanging on the windows and the glass bending, but unbroken, made the sight stranger still. Now I understood why Conrad did not even try to explain what had happened, because he couldn't. I had to see the situation for myself to make any sort of sense of it.

The inner part of the house had collapsed, the first floor falling into the cellar, with the second and third floors following behind. The outside walls remained standing but were really just empty shells. I pointed out to the people standing in front of the house that it was dangerous there, as the bulge could easily collapse at any moment and spill debris onto the street. Nobody took any heed of what I was saying. They all just looked at me as if I was foolish to suggest such a thing. Conrad chuckled, and said, 'Oh, well. Be it on their own heads! Let's go and find everyone.' With that, we walked off and left them to it.

Our parents and Gary were at the house of a family friend who also lived in Grant Place. We squeezed our way through a throng of neighbours and strangers to get into the house. Once inside, there were even more people crowding into the sitting room. We heard Mamma's voice coming from somewhere among them but we could not see her. Pushing our way through, we found her sitting in the middle of them – crying. Dad and Gary were sitting quietly beside her. Amongst the confusion of people, I quickly noted that at least one was a newspaper reporter, and some of the others were from the Corporation. Although my parents owned their home and had just finished paying off their mortgage, they were offered a Corporation house on an estate. Mamma didn't want to live 'miles away', as she put it, but settled instead for a miscellaneous, four-bedroom property about a mile away and just around the corner from my house in the Potternewton area. They were rehoused the same day.

None of us could really form an opinion of the new house on first seeing it, as that luxury was denied because of the circumstances. Curiously, this house was almost identical to the one in Grant Place. The staircases were steep and went up through the centre of it in just the same way. The only real difference was that this house in Potternewton had a bay window at the front and the rooms were smaller, with the exception of the kitchen, which was just as large as the one in Grant Place.

It was impossible for anyone to live in the new house straight away. It was in a great need of decorating, and the few saved possessions from the old house amounted to little more than a miserable damp heap in the middle of the kitchen floor. These meagre belongings, covered in a thick coating of wet soot and dust, were only recovered because a previous occupier of the house in Grant Place during the Second World War had the presence of mind to build a small air-raid shelter in the cellar beneath the kitchen part of the house. Fortunately, it was never removed after the war was over. I'm sure that person, whoever they were, would have been pleased to know that their effort was not wasted because the shelter worked, albeit many years later. It held up the floor long enough for my family to escape.

Conrad and I spent the rest of the day together working out where everyone was going to stay until thing were sorted. And during this time I was told more about the events leading up the collapse of the house. It turned out that the evening before, Edmond's wife Sandra, her mother, and their three children were visiting my mother. It got late and the children were tired, so they decided to stay over. Amanda was now six years old. It was around six-thirty in the morning when Amanda was awoken (she claimed later that it

Left: Edmond with Amanda and her brothers Mark and Darren.

Opposite: The *Yorkshire Evening Post* article from 14 August 1967.

was her baby friend who woke her). She saw a big crack in the wall behind the bedhead and heard the house rumbling. Frightened, she shook her mother to wake her. Sandra, who didn't awake fully immediately, told Amanda to go back to sleep as it was only thunder she'd heard. Amanda would not accept this and persisted, using her fingers to prise her mother's eyes open. After this, Sandra had no choice but to heed her and get up. She was horrified to see into Freddie's house next door through the crack in the wall. She hurried downstairs and opened the door to the front room – to discover that the floor had fallen into the cellar. Quickly, she raised the alarm for everyone to get out as fast as they could.

Conrad, who had been sleeping in my old attic room, became trapped behind the door leading to the attic stairs. He was prevented from opening it because the doorframe had become askew as the walls shifted. Dad freed Conrad by kicking the door in to dislodge it. Fortunately, no one was seriously injured. Dad was the only one to be slightly hurt, with a bruised elbow: he'd fallen on the stairs as they twisted sideways under him as he fled. Everyone else escaped safely as the house collapsed behind them.

Whilst bricks were falling around their heads, brave friends and neighbours risked serious injuries to themselves by going in amongst the ruins to salvage as much as they could for my parents. My family was most grateful for their efforts.

Sandra and the children returned to their own home later that morning. Later, when the events became clear, Amanda was hailed as a little heroine, and had her photograph published in a national newspaper.

Nine escape as floor of Leeds house caves in

Nine people escaped from a terrace house between Grant Place and Grant Street, Leeds 7, today shortly before the first floor collapsed.

They were warned by six-year-old Amanda Slater, who awoke to f nd the walls caving in.

In the house were Mr Arthur Slater and his wife Edna, their sons Conrad (18) and Gary (10)—the occupiers of the house—their daughter-in-law Mrs Sandra Slater (23) and her mother, Mrs. Winifred Shepherd, and three children, Amanda (6), Daren (3), and Mark (2).

Mr. and Mrs. Slater have just bought the house and were to go on holiday on Wednesday to Ireland.

LIKE THUNDER

Mrs. Slater, who is visiting them, said that she thought the noise was thunder at first.

"Amanda said it wasn't," she said. "She said, ' No. The walls weren't like that last night.'

"We ran out of the house and the floor collapsed. As we came out I saw a gap under the door. "We'd all have been in there if Amanda hadn't warned us."

Police were later keeping people away from the house and the neighbouring houses on each side, which were unoccupied.

GAP FOR FLOOR

From Grant Place the only sign of damage was a broken window and missing chimney stack, but from the other side of the house—in Grant Street —daylight could be seen through the ground floor window, together with a gap where the floor had been.

The floor itself could be seen sloping down towards the ground through the windows of the house next door.

A Leeds Corporation spokesman said that surveyors would be inspecting the damage to see whether there was any risk to other houses in the row.

Mr. Slater and his family are being rehoused.

Grant Street as it is now.

Looking down what was Grant Street from Roundhay Road.

Freddie and Betty had left the area some weeks before and their house was standing empty, so there was no danger to them. A policeman stood guard over the house in Grant Place for a few days to prevent looters from going into the ruins, which enabled a few more items to be saved. One of them was my Grandfather Walter's tin trunk. A cat had somehow managed to get itself trapped in the ruins of the cellar, and was safely rescued a couple of days later when its cries were heard. I thought it was a little odd that the saga of living in this house began and ended with a story of a 'trapped cat'.

Everything was topsy-turvy for a time. Mamma took herself and Gary off to Ireland to her sister Della's house. She was suffering from the traumatic effect of all that had happened. The rest of us worked very hard to get the new house habitable before she returned. The entire house needed to be decorated and furnished.

The official statement said the collapse was an act of God – more like an act of the Devil, in my view. On this, the insurance people would not pay my parents, so they received no help from them. The only money that did come forward was a payment for the rateable value of the land that the house stood on, but that was almost lost when a bill from the Corporation came demanding money for propping up the shell of the house. Later, this bill was withdrawn after my mother protested at the stupidity and meanness of it.

The St Vincent de Paul Society from St Augustine's church, Leeds, helped tremendously in providing some bedroom furniture. Fortunately, my parents had savings, so in a relatively short time, considering the circumstances, we got things together.

In the meantime, the house in Grant Place caught fire twice, and a large crack developed from underneath a bedroom window and ran along the length of six other houses, so the residents of those houses had to leave as well. The whole street was later demolished.

The area has since become a small industrial estate. A building belonging to Asgha Hosiery Co., Roundhay Road was built on the site of the street and partly covers the ground that the house was built on.

Seven

A NEW START

In March 1968, Tony and I became the proud parents of our son Alan, whom we named after Tony's father. By this time, my family had settled into their house and were getting on with their lives, trying to replace everything they had lost. Some items were, of course, impossible to replace.

My father had stopped working away by request. He had come to a time in his life when he'd had enough of travelling about the country. He managed to get a position in Leeds, which enabled him to carry on doing the same work as before, but now in local government buildings. It meant shorter working hours and a cut in pay, but he didn't mind this too much, as he was able to manage.

The house in Grant Place was gone forever, and, as far as I was concerned, so were the ghosts, buried deep and squashed into the ground. At last, we were all living a normal life. Months later, whilst out shopping, I unexpectedly ran into Marilyn, an old friend of Gail's and mine. She used to live in a street at the bottom of Grant Place. Because our lives took different turns as we grew up, we had both lost contact with most friends of our own age. After a long chat in the street, catching up with each other's news, we discovered that we were living very near to one another again. She too had a baby; a girl called Adel, who was almost the same age as Alan. The timely meeting rekindled a friendship that became closer than it had been before. We saw each other frequently, usually during the day, spending our time taking the children to the park on fine days, or doing our shopping together. Marilyn also knew my mother and occasionally would call at her house for a few minutes before coming to mine. My mother was very fond of Marilyn and enjoyed her visits. We were all very comfortable with each other and the way things were.

Mamma hardly showed any interest in the local shops and could not get out of the habit of shopping in town. She enjoyed it really, and it got her out of the house. One such morning, Mamma called to my house as usual. She was cheerful and chatty as she normally was, with a big bag slung over one arm, and her new shopping trolley. They seemed to be all the rage at the time, and it was a perfect item for her to have; she thought they were a great idea. 'I wished I'd had one years ago,' she said. A short time later she took her leave and set off to her friend Kathleen's house, which was about half a mile or so down the road. She generally caught the bus to town from a bus stop nearest to Kathleen's home.

I stood at my gate holding Alan in my arms and waved her off. I watched her go and noted the empty shopping trolley zigzagging behind her as she pulled it along, then she disappeared from view. It brought a smile to my face to think how pleased she'd been over a simple thing like that. I turned and went back into the house. I expected her to return in around three hour's time.

No sooner had I closed the door behind me and settled Alan into his chair, when I spotted Marilyn through the window. She was coming down the street heading towards my house. Her face looked blank, and with her lips tight, I could see immediately that something was wrong. A moment or so later, I opened the door to her and she walked in. I stepped back to allow her to pass through to my living room. She was upset and angry.

'I've just been to see your mother, but she wouldn't answer the door to me.' Her voice was shaking.

'That's because she's not in.'

'She is in!' she insisted with her voice now raised. 'I saw her look at me through the bedroom window – twice. And she moved the curtain.'

My mother.

'But she couldn't have. She's gone to town.' Then, stupidly, I asked, 'Are you sure you went to the right house?'

'Of course I did!' she snapped. 'Do you think I'm daft or something?'

'No, I don't.'

I never once thought that she was daft: far from it. And I'd never seen her angry like this before. I was sure a simple explanation could be found, but I was bamboozled as to what it might be.

'Are you sure it was my mother that you saw? Did you try the door? You know she always leaves it unlocked when she's in!'

'I saw her through the net curtain; it was definitely a woman – who else could it be?' Her eyes flickered away from me then she added, 'I did try the door: it was locked.'

Everything was wrong about this. I knew my mother could not possibly have been in the house when Marilyn called. And Marilyn was definitely no idiot. I became worried that she may have seen a burglar. It was the only explanation I could find.

'Will you keep your eye on Alan for me? I'll go and check the house – just in case someone has broken in.'

'Err… yes!'

I could see by the sulky expression on her face that she didn't think that was necessary. But I knew it was. I had a key to the back door. I also had a very large Alsatian bitch called Cleo. I took her with me.

Me and Cleo in the 1960s.

There was no sign of a break-in from the back of the house. But I still cautiously unlocked the door and went inside. Everything was still and silent, except for the inevitable particles of dust exposed by a ray of sunlight forcing its way through the kitchen window. I stood and looked around. Straining my ears, I listened for the slightest noise. The kitchen had a warm and pleasant air of tranquillity about it. I called out and made as much noise as I could to shatter the calm. I wanted any would-be intruders to know that I was there, so I could give them the chance to escape before I began my search. I didn't want any surprises. I stood still for a few moments and listened again, but the house was completely quiet.

Sending Cleo in first, we searched every room thoroughly, including the cellar. If anyone had been there, hiding, Cleo would have sniffed him or her out. She obeyed my every command. I looked to see if anything had fallen against the bedroom window that might have given Marilyn the impression that someone was there. I found nothing at all to explain the woman at the window. I locked up and returned home.

Marilyn expected some sort of explanation from me when I got back. I couldn't give her one. She looked at me with suspicion when I told her that there was nobody in the house. Shortly after, she left.

It was around 3.30 p.m. when my mother returned. 'I've got some lovely lamb chops, Colette!' she said, as she battled her way through my door with her big bulging bag, and a now-heavy shopping trolley. Before mentioning Marilyn and the house, I let her sort out the shopping and paid her for the chops.

'Mam, did you go back home, just after you left here this morning to go to town?'

'No, of course not,' then asked with suspicion. 'Why should you ask that?'

After I'd told her what Marilyn had said, she was afraid to go home alone. I could not convince her that everything was okay. She only left when I suggested that she took Cleo with her. Cleo was very happy to oblige.

Everything in the house was as my mother had left it. We could never find an explanation for Marilyn's experience. Regardless of what I said to her, I could not alter her suspicions against my mother and she never visited her again. A good friendship was spoiled forever.

There were the odd times when I had thought that all was not as it should be in the house in Potternewton. But I tried to dismiss these thoughts from my mind. I could not accept any possibility that there could be anything wrong with this house, ghost-wise. I told myself that if something was amiss, then it had to be imaginary. How could it be anything else? Trying to explain it away to myself, I was satisfied that the reason I sometime had these ideas was because the house bore such a strong resemblance to the one in Grant Place.

Then Tony accepted a job with ICI as an overseer in a textile mill in Port Elizabeth, South Africa. It was as if the world had ended for my mother when I told her. Dad and Tony's parents appeared to take the news better, but we knew they were hurting inside just as much as Mamma was, but she was not very good at hiding her emotions.

Alan was now two years old. He was my in-laws' first grandchild, and we'd just discovered that we had a second baby on the way. This made the news even harder for them because they would not be able to see their new grandchild or Alan growing up.

Our house was put up for sale and Mamma cried every time she saw the 'For Sale' sign attached to a post outside the front door. Before leaving England in August 1970, Tony had

Me and Tony with a young Alan. This photograph was taken just before we left for South Africa.

to work in Ilfracombe, Devon, for a few months to train for his new job. This helped to give our families time to get used to the idea of us leaving. But it was still very upsetting when we said goodbye. It was one of the hardest things I'd ever had to do. Mamma could not face our leaving day, so she went to Ireland for a few days to avoid it.

We liked South Africa. It was a big, beautiful country, but I did miss everyone. On the third of December 1970, Tony's father came to visit. He had previously suffered a stroke and the long journey had taken a lot out of him. When we went to pick him up from the airport, he was edgy and cantankerous. On the fifteenth of December, our beautiful daughter Julia was born. I then missed my family even more, although I was always kept up to date with the latest news from the numerous letters I received from everyone, and my father-in-law filled us in with extra bits. The journey and the heat had proved to be too much for my father-in-law: he collapsed and spent three days in hospital. So instead of staying for three months as planned, he decided to return to England on Christmas Day, now that he had satisfied himself that all was well with his grandson, Alan. And he had the bonus of seeing his new granddaughter, Julia.

It did not feel one bit like Christmas when Tony and I took him to the airport for his noonday flight to Johannesburg. It was hot and the sun was shining. At the airport, my father-in-law kissed his grandchildren and muttered a goodbye. It was very sad. Then he turned and walked away without as much as a glance back in our direction. We quietly watched him cross the tarmac to board the aeroplane. The wind suddenly came up from nowhere as it often did in Port Elizabeth; the locals knew it as the windy city. He pressed on with his head bent as he struggled to walk against the wind, which looked as if it was trying to blow him back and prevent him from leaving. Something about this scene told us this would be the last time that we'd see him, and it was. He died almost three months later, soon after Alan's third birthday, in March 1971.

His death made us realise just how far away and cut off we were from our families. Almost two weeks had gone by before we found out that he'd died. It seemed very wrong that Tony had missed his own father's funeral, and we felt that we should have been at home.

The following December, Janet, Tony's sister, came to stay with us for a holiday. I was really pleased that Alan still remembered her, but the seeds of a worry were planted that he would forget her and the rest of our family in time, and Julia would never even know them. After discussing this, Tony and I thought it was more important for our children to know their extended family and be part of them. With this thought in mind, we planned to return to England.

Tony was afraid of flying and I could not bear the thought of spending a month on a ship. I hated the smell of stale air below deck; it made me feel sick. The only solution to resolve our travel problems was for me and the children to fly back to England, and for Tony to follow later by ship.

I knew things would not be quite the same as before in England and I would no longer fit into the same slot that I came out of. I had not expected time to stand still while we'd been away. And in all that time, not once, did anyone mention anything about the house in Potternewton – nor did I expect them to, other than it was arranged for us to stay there until we got our own house.

We arrived at Heathrow Airport on 14 December 1972. Mamma had put us up in her bedroom because it was the largest in the house. She'd moved Dad out of it and into a small back bedroom. He was easy-going and did not seem to mind. Alan and I slept together in my parent's double bed. My mother slept in the same room, in a single bed. In between, near the foot of both beds, she placed a cot for Julia. We were all very comfortable.

I did not want her to go to all this trouble and would have been quite happy to sleep in what used to be Conrad's bedroom, but my mother would not hear of it. She said it was a cold room, and as we had just left an African summer behind, she thought the sudden change to winter might affect us. On the contrary, the cold didn't bother us at all, even though it was December; we found the artificial heat from gas fires and central heating systems to be very uncomfortable at first. Things were made worse when everyone wanted to turn up the heat for us, thinking we might be cold. This made me feel stifled and I had to frequently go outdoors for air. I had become used to a natural and different kind of heat.

I did find it difficult at first to judge the time of day because it never seemed to become full daylight. This really confused my built-in body clock; it took weeks to correct itself.

Dad and Mam at Conrad's wedding (Conrad married during our time in South Africa).

Eight

THE HOUSE IN POTTERNEWTON

Mamma had taken to going to Morning Mass almost every day. Three days after our arrival, she rose early and tried to get out of bed as quietly as possible in order not to wake the children or myself. She was not quiet enough and woke us all up. The children followed her down the stairs. As I contemplated rising myself, I listened to Alan's tireless chatter drifting up from the kitchen. I knew that once the children were up, there was no staying in bed for me.

A few minutes later, I heard Mamma's voice cry out in alarm as she realised that it was getting late. 'Oh, it's ten to nine, I have to dash,' she said to the children. 'Go back upstairs to your mother.' On hearing this I was shocked, because I found it hard to believe that it was that late; I was convinced it could only be around seven-thirty. The clock was on the far side of a chest of drawers that had been positioned between the two beds. I couldn't see the clock face because it was turned away from me. In order to reach it, I slid the top half of my body out of the bed, placing one hand on the floor to support myself. I stretched out as far as I could and just managed to grasp the clock with my fingertips and turn it around. It was indeed ten minutes to nine o'clock.

Mamma ushered the children onto the stairs as she said goodbye to them. I heard her plant a big wet kiss on each of them in turn. I really had to get up now, even though I did not want to. I retracted my body back towards the bed in order to straighten up – and as I did so, from out of nowhere, a baby appeared on my mother's bed with its head facing towards the foot. It was aged somewhere between twelve and eighteen months and was naked except for a linen nappy. It laughed as it bounced back and forth on its hands and knees having a wonderful time. It was quite a big baby and it did not have much hair, and, although I could not be certain, it looked to me like a baby boy.

I could not believe it, and wondered where it came from. I was still stretched out with both hands on the floor when it bounced too close to the edge of the bed and toppled off. I instantly reacted by trying to catch it, but it disappeared before hitting the floor. I backed into the bed as fast as I could, only to see a horrid, scrawny little man crouching at the bottom of Julia's cot with his elbows resting on the frame. He was watching me through small, sinister black eyes. He smirked mischievously to expose a full set of ugly brown teeth. He was chewing something: tobacco, I guessed. His face was covered in soot.

Dirty black hair, in need of cutting, stuck out from underneath a black leather peaked cap. He was dressed in a not very clean, tight-fitting black suit. Under his jacket, he wore a high-buttoned waistcoat. A greasy maroon cravat was knotted tightly around his thin neck, but did not quite cover a grubby white collarless shirt. I judged him to be around forty years old.

In spite of my amazement, I was momentarily distracted from his face when a small feather, or a tuft of fluff, caught my eye as it gently fell to the carpet from his shoulder. Alan and Julia had not reached the top of the stairs yet. I could hear them talking to each other, with Alan doing most of it. I wanted to call out to tell them not to come into the room, but at the same time, I wanted them to come in quickly. Instead, I remained speechless. I lay as near to the edge of the bed as I could without toppling out.

Someone standing just an inch or so away from my face suddenly blocked my view. I moved my head back and looked up to see a woman standing there with her arms folded and her behind propped up against the chest of drawers. She looked very much at home. She glanced down at me from over her shoulder, with an expression of total indifference, as if I did not count one iota. Her build was bigger than that of the man's, and they both looked to be around the same age. Her paisley patterned wrap-round apron was in two shades of blue and grey. Under it she wore a creamy-coloured short-sleeved jumper. I was unable to tell from the angle I was at if her fair hair was short or tied back. Curiously, she bore some resemblance to my mother's sister, Della.

The baby did not reappear, but both the man and the woman remained in the room and continued to look at me until the very moment that Alan opened the door. Only then did they fade out of sight, leaving me with the impression that they had come to see me, perhaps because I'd been away so long.

I leaped out of bed and rapidly dressed, then scampered down the stairs with the children following. I pretended to play a game of 'tig' with them. They were not quite sure what the game was, but tried to play along with me anyway.

I slung open the front and back doors of the house for an easy escape if needed. Tentatively, I then stood at the bottom of the stairs. With eyes and ears fully alert, I looked and listened for them. Alan came and stood beside me and also looked up the stairs. He screwed up his face as he tried to figure out the rules of this new game. He turned and looked up at me as if I was daft.

Then we heard them walking away, upwards. They sounded as if they were wearing clogs and climbing a bare wooden spiral staircase. Although the footsteps went upwards, they were not coming from the same place as the existing stairwells, but somewhere in the space above them. Alan now became afraid and clung to my hand. In a small shaky voice, he asked, 'Who's there, Mammy? Who's there?'

I could not answer him, because I did not know what to say even though all kinds of thoughts crossed my mind. But not one of them made any sense. I was still trying to disbelieve what my eyes had just witnessed upstairs in the bedroom and what my ears were listening to at this very moment. 'God! This cannot be true!' But I knew it was.

I ruffled Alan's curls under my fingers and moved him away from the foot of the stairs. I attempted to distract him by changing the subject and closing the doors. For the next ten minutes or so, off and on, we continued to hear the clunking footsteps as they continued to

Drawings of the couple I saw in the bedroom.

climb the unseen stairs. I pretended that nothing was happening and carried on as normal, whilst at the same time keeping my ears pricked and making sure we stayed downstairs.

An hour later Mamma returned. In a whisper, so I would not alarm the children, I told her briefly about the goings on while she was out. Afterwards, the children went outside to play in the yard, and then I was able to speak freely. Mamma sat at the kitchen table and listened fearfully when I told her about the people I'd seen. She put her face in her hands and took a deep breath. Then she spoke at last: 'Yes, I know something is here. It's horrible and unbelievable to think of, but the ghosts have followed us from the other house!' She blinked across at me through the gaps in her fingers, and then shook her head. 'Conrad had a terrible time of it in his bedroom – that's why I didn't want you to sleep in it; I was thinking about the children.' She went on and explained, 'Something kept lying on him – a big weight. That happened to others too!' Again I was speechless, and tried to unravel all this crazy stuff in my mind, but to no avail.

Later, I was to speak of the house with Uncle Tigue, my mother's brother. He too complained about the terrible weight that bore down on him when he stayed at the house for a time. He said it felt as if someone was kneeling on his chest. He was too afraid to go to bed at times, and would just sit on the end of it with the window wide open.

I thought hard about what was going on and tried to get some answers to it all by attempting to put some pieces together. I started with the woman to see if I could figure out where she fitted in with all this. Until now, I'd not considered that a woman may also have been haunting the house in Grant Place. I came to the conclusion that many of the objects that had gone missing in the past were the sort of thing that a woman, rather than a man, would take an interest in, such as the baby clothes and my hairbrush. And a woman was very likely responsible for many of the other strange things that happened there, like the sweeping of the floors that Conrad used to hear. Brideen once accused me of taking her lipstick from her locked cupboard, saying I must have picked the lock. I was totally innocent of this; I had never once tried to get into her cupboard. But I did wonder how on earth her lipstick had gone missing.

Then, coming back to this house, I recalled the woman at the window that my friend Marilyn said she had seen. Other things leapt into my mind now: not only a woman, but also a baby! A baby was connected to Grant Place. Then there was the man. I wondered if the one I saw here was the same man that Conrad had seen in the other house, watching the doorway of the attic stairs. If this was so, then the 'ghosts' had somehow moved from one house to the other. It just had to be. The chances of this house being so haunted in its own right were far too much of a coincidence. Most people would never live in one haunted house in their lives, let alone two!

I believed the ghosts must have been carried here, but in what? So few items were saved. I found it difficult to come up with any one thing in particular. I had no evidence, only a gut feeling that it was my grandfather Walter's old tin trunk that was responsible. I had been puzzled as to how it got here in this house, because the last time I saw it was in the middle of the street of Grant Place, days after the house fell down. I just happened to be passing by at the top of the street when I spotted it. I had left clothes in it when I first left the house to move into my own. I was curious to see if they were still there. I detoured my way down the street and looked inside it and found it empty. A policeman who was still standing guard over the house came over to me and asked what I was up to. I explained who I was, and he let me be. An hour or two later, when I passed by on my way home, it was gone. I thought the policeman must have removed it from the middle of the road or the refuse collectors had taken it. I though no more about it until I saw it once more in the house at Potternewton on my return from South Africa.

After I had my good 'think' about the ghosts, I tried to shrug off any further thoughts about them. I had enough on my mind right now and too much to do. I had to make a new home for my family, so ghosts had no place in my life. I was in the mind that if I gave them no heed then they would go away. Who was I trying to kid? Only me! We could not escape the ghosts while we were still under the same roof as them.

I had recently received a letter from Tony. He couldn't get an early passage on a ship. The 'Castle Shipping Lines' were fully booked. So, unless he decided to travel by air instead, he was not going to return to Leeds for months. He made his choice to sail. I had no option but to house hunt for us alone. In the meantime, the children and I continued to stay with my parents.

Julia had never been a nervous child: in fact, I would go as far as to say that she was quite the opposite. She rarely cried and was always happy to go to bed, and had no misgivings about the dark. Therefore, I was very alarmed shortly after I'd put her to bed one evening to hear her screaming for the first time in her life.

I ran up the stairs as fast as I could, with my father following behind. As I barged into the bedroom, I switched on the light. Julia was cowering and curled up on her pillow.

It was clear that she was very distressed. She uncurled herself and pointed to the foot of the cot. Then a look of surprise came over her face when she saw that it was empty. In her disbelief, she searched and patted around the cot, making it obvious that she had experienced something being in the cot with her. Frightened and bewildered, she reached her small arms out to me. It took a lot of reassurance and coaxing her before she settled back down to sleep. Twice more, over the next two weeks, the same thing happened. But that wasn't the only problem she had to contend with.

One morning after breakfast, Mamma and I were busy washing and drying the dishes. Alan was sitting on the floor playing with his toy cars. Julia wandered into the hall. She had taken to playing at the bottom of the stairs, which were a novelty to her as she wasn't used to stairs; back in Port Elizabeth we had lived on one level.

A few minutes had gone by when, from upstairs, Julia's screams ripped through the air. Fearing that she'd had an accident, the three of us rushed to her aid. I reached the foot of the stairs first and looked up to see her standing near the top, clutching the uprights of the bannister. She was peering through the rungs of the bannister into the small back bedroom. Her small body was stiff, as if frozen. Her eyes widened, and she became hysterical with fear. Never before had I heard such screams of complete terror. Her small legs gave a little skip, and then she threw herself down the stairs. Fortunately, I was there to catch her.

It was heartbreaking to see such a young child so afraid. Mamma could not contain her anger and darted upstairs to the bedroom. I followed her with Julia in my arms. Mamma shook her fist in the air and yelled, 'You dirty coward for terrorising a baby!' This brought back an acute memory of Gail doing a similar thing, but this time it was not remotely funny.

We searched the room but found nothing. Julia, through her sobs, could only say she saw a 'nasty doggy'. This did not help us much, as she used the term 'doggy' to describe anything that she didn't know the name of. I knew she was not necessarily describing something that resembled a dog, because she called a canine a dog and she loved them as she did any other animal that she came across. I had never before seen her afraid of any animal, large or small.

I gave her a pen and paper to see if she could draw what she had seen. She tried very hard to do so, but she was too young and was unable to draw anything other than a rough circle. I went through every logical and illogical thing that I could think of with her to try and discover what she had seen. She shook her head every time at all my suggestions and drawings. Yet she did hesitate, but just for a moment, to study a rough drawing of a man that I did, and then shook her head once more. I really wanted to know what she had seen in the bedroom that day, but whatever it was, I was never to discover.

Almost every time Mamma went down to the cellar or anywhere in the house, the children trailed behind her. They took a lot of interest in everything she did and it gave them an excuse to explore the house at the same time. Mamma stored the vegetables in the cellar, just as she did in the house in Grant Place. The cellar door and steps were in the exact same position as in the old house. I watched as the three of them, in turn, reappeared through the door on their return to the kitchen. First came Mamma, carrying a cabbage and potatoes. Alan followed, carrying onions. There was a slight delay before Julia appeared. When she did, she came rushing into view, and at the same time, gave a little hop as if something pinched her behind. She arched her back and fearfully looked over her shoulder.

In a flurry she turned and reversed into the kitchen. She did not speak, and quickly came to my side. Standing with her fingers in her mouth, she quietly studied the open doorway.

I could see myself doing the same thing when I lived in Grant Place, and knew instantly by her reactions what she had experienced on the cellar steps and I did not like it at all. Although Julia had bad encounters with the 'thing' in the house, it did not have a lasting effect on her. Being as young as she was, she quickly forgot them and put them behind her, which I was pleased about.

All our plans to buy a house or anything else on our return to Leeds were dashed when I received a letter from Tony, telling me the devastating news that his chequebook had been stolen a week before and we'd lost all our money. After the children and I left South Africa, Tony had moved out of our flat because we had sold all our furniture. He went to lodge at a friend's house until he was to leave the country also. To accumulate as much money as possible while he could, he had taken on an extra job in the evenings serving behind a bar, and was able to live on the extra money without touching his main wage other than sending me some money each month. We estimated that we should have had enough money for a deposit on a house, or at least enough to furnish a house by the time he was to leave the country.

Tony had left his chequebook in a pocket of a jacket, which was hanging in the wardrobe of his room. He was asked to leave the door to his room open while he was at work in order for it to be cleaned. Unknown to him, another chap who was staying in the house was a thief. He took the chequebook and left. Tony never saw the man again, but his cheques were being cashed all over the place. The thief was somehow able to draw cash from the bank. He bought jewellery, expensive clothes, and paid for hotel bills from our money. The bank refused to compensate Tony for his loss because he hadn't reported the chequebook as stolen straight away. He did not know it was missing until he wanted to send me some money, but by then it was too late: most of our money was gone. Tony argued with the bank that an identity card with a photograph on it was required in order to cash cheques, and the bank had allowed transactions to take place without one being shown. After he pointed out this total incompetence by the staff, he was compensated for only the last cheque cashed. In all, the thief left us with around £400. We were devastated.

The police knew who the man was, but his whereabouts were unknown. He was leaving a trail of cashed cheques as he moved from town to town. It was only a matter of time before the police would catch up with him. However, it was too late for us: our money was now gone and catching the thief would not bring it back. This was one of the unhappiest times of my life.

It was July 1973 before Tony could return to Leeds. By this time, I had left my parent's house and moved to the Crossgates area of Leeds. The house I'd rented wasn't really what I wanted, but I thought it would do for a year or so until we could sort things out.

Whilst we were in South Africa, Conrad and his wife, Catherine, had gone to live in Ireland. They had left some furniture stored at my parent's house just in case things did not work out over there and wanted to return. Instead, they stayed and offered the furniture to me, which I accepted gratefully. Because I had never met Catherine or their children, I paid them a visit.

Jokingly, I asked Conrad if the furniture was contaminated with ghosts and if that was why he didn't want it. He jested that it could be. He then changed his tone and blurted out, 'I've seen the same horrible man in the cellar of the house in Potternewton that I'd previously seen in Grant Place. This time though, the man seemed to be afraid of me and ran away.' It was usually difficult to get Conrad to talk about the ghosts in any detail because he was afraid to do so, as I was. So it wasn't discussed very often. We felt as if it would somehow come back if we spoke of it. Nevertheless, he told me that something had followed him to Ireland, and he terrified me when he said it caused him to levitate from his bed. Catherine confirmed this and said, 'I was wakened by his screams and was horrified to see him floating above the bed with his face almost touching the ceiling.'

This was the most that Conrad and I had ever spoken about the ghosts in one go before. Conrad was visibly shaken during our brief discussion on the subject. To eliminate some of his fear, and mine, I mentioned my thoughts on how privileged we really were to have encountered these things and to know that there are such things as ghosts when most people could only guess about them. He was delighted with my philosophy, and agreed with me wholeheartedly. This gave him the confidence to continue with our talk. He went on to tell me that while I was living in South Africa, and before he married Catherine, Laura came home to Leeds for a visit. As always, she stayed with our parents. It was her first stay in the house in Potternewton. Late one night, she was sleeping soundly in the small back bedroom when someone running noisily up the stairs, across the landing and up the attic stairs disturbed her. She assumed it was Conrad, because he slept in one of the attic bedrooms, and she was annoyed at his lack of consideration. Moments later, the bedroom light was switched on, then off again. Again, she thought it had to be Conrad acting the fool and became angry with him.

Conrad.

My mother, sister Laura and her son Gary.

Although Laura has a good sense of fun, she will not put up with silliness, especially at such a late hour when she is trying to sleep. She was like our mother: small in stature, but with a big temper – if annoyed enough, she could cause an earthquake. Conrad knew not to trifle with her. Laura woke the whole household with her screams when she felt a heavy weight leap on her, leading her to believe she was under attack. She furiously fought the weight off and managed to get out of the bed and turn on the light, only to find that she was alone in the room. Everyone in the house came rushing to her aid, including Conrad. He strongly denied running up the stairs or anywhere – and he certainly had not entered her room.

Even though Laura knew that nobody was in her room when she turned on the light, it took a lot to convince her that a trick had not been played on her. She still remembers the incident vividly, and accepts that the second house was also strange.

Nine

THE ACCIDENT

Julia had started school for the first time in the summer of 1975. I got a job as a part-time barmaid at a pub opposite the school that both she and Alan attended. It was so convenient for me that I didn't need a childminder. I was able to pick them up myself at home time because I finished at three thirty as well. All I had to do was cross the road to them. I enjoyed working behind the bar and meeting so many different people. Things were beginning to go well for us, our life was coming together at last, and we dared to make plans for buying our future home. But alas, one cold morning in November, things changed and all our plans were quashed.

I was dressed and just about to wake the children up for school when a knock sounded on the door. Tony had already left for work and I didn't expect him to call back home for anything. It must be the postman, I told myself. 'Hold on a minute,' I called out, as I realized that Tony had locked the door behind him. I found my key. A moment later I was at the door and opened it. I was amazed to see my father standing there with his head held down. His hands were stuffed deep down into his overcoat pockets. He was buttoned up high, with a scarf wrapped tightly around his neck and pulled up in an attempt to cover his ears. He was hatless, which was unusual for him at this time of the year. His face was grey and grim. I knew instantly that something was very, very wrong. Without speaking, he walked in.

'Dad! What is it, what are you doing here at this time?' I was fearful of his answer.

'Your mother's had an accident.'

'What! A bad one?' He nodded and I felt sick. We both sat down. 'Tell me what's happened.'

He looked at me and his face became even greyer. I expected him to tell me that she was dead.

'She's been knocked down – the car ran over her.' His words echoed through my head. 'She's very badly hurt. She could die,' he sobbed. A few moments passed before I could speak.

'But how did it happen?'

Julia and Alan, pictured while still at primary school.

'It was last night. She'd gone to her friend's house – Eileen. I was tired and went to bed early and read a book, but I fell asleep. The police wakened me at eleven thirty. They told me that a car had hit her and the driver stopped and that there were witnesses. I was so shocked I can't remember everything they said.'

'Did it happen on her way to Eileen's or on her way home?'

'It had to be on her way home, because it was late. I can't remember the time. I've been up all night. The police took me to St James's hospital, and then they went away. She was moved to Chapel Allerton hospital through the night for some reason, I think because of her head injuries – she's in intensive care.'

I was numb with shock, and I almost forgot to get the children up and ready for school. By the time my father and I went to the hospital later that morning, I had passed the bad news to the rest of the family.

I prepared myself mentally for the worst outcome, and tried to accept the fact that Mamma could die at any moment. She was in a coma. Apart from sustaining serious head injuries, she also suffered a broken pelvic, and cuts and bruises. Dad, Alfred and I visited her every day. Brideen and her daughter Terrien travelled up from the Isle of Wight. Her husband Deitor stayed behind. He had now left the Army and was working as a prison officer on the island. After a few days, Brideen and Terrien returned home.

Mamma was in the coma for three long months. When she woke up, it was apparent that she had suffered some brain damage. She was left an invalid, with her life cruelly destroyed from then on, thus causing an adverse effect on our lives as well.

We were never to discover the circumstances of the accident, or get any further information other than what my father had already been told by the police the night of the accident. There was never a court case or anything else to throw any light on it.

My father was due to retire the September following the accident, but this had to be brought forward because Mamma needed to be taken care of. In reality, he didn't retire: his work was well cut out for him after Mamma was dismissed from the hospital and came home. It was different work from what he'd been used to, and he found it tough. He had to learn quickly how to be a housewife and a nurse without ever having done anything like it before. He also had to learn how to cook and shop for groceries. It was a very difficult time for him – I helped all I could. Mamma needed care day and night and she was very difficult to handle. Dad wasn't given any help other than mine, so I had to give up my little job. Our lives truly had been turned upside down.

At the time of Mamma's accident she was quite well known through the church, and from running around doing good deeds for people. She knew a lot of people and had many friends. The switchboard at the hospital repeatedly became jammed with people making enquires about her. After she was out of danger, the waiting room was filled with her visitors, most unknown to my father or me. There were even days when I was not permitted on the ward to see her because she already had more visitors around her bed than she was allowed. I could only peer into the ward and wonder who most of them were – so much so that the hospital staff thought that she was a celebrity and complained to my father and I for not warning them!

A few months after Mamma's accident, a letter and a box of chocolates came from Ireland for her. They were from a gentleman named Jack Higgins. I read the letter to her. He had heard about her accident and was writing to wish her well. He remembered her from when he was a child: she was a few years older than he was, and terrified the residents of Thomondgate, Limerick (where she lived when she was young) by galloping bareback on her horse up the High Road, doing acrobatics on its back. She had told me in the past of having dreams of being in a circus and thought if she was good enough her father would let her join one, which he never did. But all was not lost, because this wildness or bravery was to pay off when she was around seventeen years old. Jack said in his letter that she was a heroine, and how he would always remember the time when she undoubtedly saved the lives of both his brother and father, and many others – 200-300 people – during a fire.

I was quite surprised at this, because I didn't readily recall ever having heard this story before. Mamma had never mentioned anything to me about it. But a vague memory came to my mind of Gary, when he was a small boy, excitedly telling me something about my mother and a fire when he returned from a trip to Limerick with her. I had not taken enough heed of what he had said, and I took it that he meant it happened whilst they were there. It could only be that Gary had heard the story of the fire whilst he was in Limerick, because Jack described it as happening in the early twenties when electricity was brought to Limerick City for the first time. Many people were working on the project above a storeroom containing oil drums and explosives. Two of the workers were Jack's father and brother. A fire developed in the storeroom and my mother had spotted it and raised the alarm. With no hesitation or regard for her own safety, she ran into the building and rolled out the drums, and dragged out boxes of explosives until help arrived. It was said that by her actions she saved many lives that day, for if an explosion had occurred, it would not only have put the workers in great danger, but it could have also destroyed Thomondgate.

I felt quite proud of my mother on reading this letter. I looked across at her sitting in the armchair next to the fire. My heart always felt heavy when I looked at her now. Her interest was more on her unsuccessful attempt to open the chocolates than the letter. Until now, I thought I knew almost everything about her, but I guess I was wrong.

'Did you get hurt or anything?' I asked her.

'What?'

'In the fire, did you get hurt?'

'No!' she answered soberly, still showing more interest in the chocolates.

'Come on, tell me something about it!' My prompting seemed to work. Her eyes widened and then she said, 'I was rewarded with £5. Some official gave it to me.' Then she laughed. 'I was given a ride on a fire engine.' It was amazing: most times since her accident, she was unable to remember what she'd eaten for her last meal, yet she was able to remember that day all those years ago.

'£5 was a lot then. What did you do with it?'

'I didn't know what to do with all that money. I'd never had that much before. I didn't want to waste it.' Her mind drifted off for a moment, then she continued. 'Everybody was poor then. I gave it to my mother, and she didn't want to take it. I made her take it, but she gave me some of it back. I can't remember how much, but I bought sweets for all the kids around. It was a great treat.' Her face beamed as she recalled her happy memory. She always got pleasure out of giving. I knew from first-hand experience that while she was running her home and raising the six of us children, she sent continuous parcels, usually of clothing or bedding, to help the families of her brother and sister in Ireland as work was not plentiful then. At the same time, back home in Leeds, she helped many people to find a home. Where she could help she did, and all at her own expense – rarely spending on herself. She even managed to do a little matchmaking too. Her tasks were endless.

The first six years following Mamma's accident were a waking nightmare for both my parents and me. They were very bleak days. To try and bring a bit of life and normality into my parents' house, I bought Dad a budgerigar for his Christmas present. We'd always had canaries or a budgie when we were young and living at home. Dad had a particular liking for them. He called the bird Peter as all the past budgies were named. It was green and scruffy and never learned to fly, although it was rarely in its cage. But it had a lovely personality for a bird. It followed my father everywhere. It even climbed all the way up the stairs to the bathroom, which must have felt like an ascent up Mount Everest to a little budgie. By the time it reached the landing, my father was almost ready to come back down. It was later discovered to be a hen, but its name remained Peter.

Afterwards, Alfred gave Mam and Dad a kitten named Tommy. The antics between the kitten and the budgie did help to make the house a cheerier place to be in, but they could not cure the situation.

Dad found it increasingly difficult to take care of Mamma. The house was totally unsuitable for an invalid. The stairs were too steep and narrow, and Dad had to carry Mamma down them on his back.

I wanted to take care of my parents myself. I would have found it much easier if we all lived in the same house or even close by. I lived 4 miles away, but I could not afford to buy a bigger house. We could not get a larger council house either, so life went on with all its difficulties as before.

We had always made a point of never mentioning the ghost problems to Mamma, as things were bad enough as they were. But almost every night she was screaming and complaining that people were in her room. She objected venomously to the presence of an ugly woman, but another, who she described as a little old man in a flat cap, she rather liked. Because of her mental state and the drugs she'd been prescribed, I took all this to be in her mind. Also, I'd had enough of the dammed ghosts, and dismissed them from my life.

One day, I bought an instamatic camera from a friend for my father; he had once mentioned that he would like one. I bought a film, but no flash, as it was a very sunny morning when I took it to him. To test it, we took photographs outside my parent's house and it worked perfectly.

Mamma was sitting in a chair in her bedroom waiting to be taken downstairs. The sun shone directly on her through the window. On the strength of this, I took the risk of taking her photograph, indoors without a flash. I took four of them, one after the other, before giving up. They turned out to be clear enough, and Mamma gave a big beaming smile on each of them. But on all of them was an unexplained white shape directly in front of her, and she appeared to be stretching to see over the top of it. It took the form of someone small and wearing a flat cap. Two of the photographs have since gone missing.

I heard some years later that my cousin, Kieran, whilst sitting at the kitchen table during a visit, saw a little old man in a flat cap enter the room from the cellar door. He walked straight through the kitchen and disappeared into the hall. Kieran asked Conrad who the old man was. 'Oh, it's just the ghost,' he answered.

Since August 1979, I'd been working part-time in the office of a well-known company. The money was good and I enjoyed the work. In the beginning, I only worked on Sundays, but within the first year, I was working almost full-time. It was easier by then because my children were getting older. I somehow managed the extra hours and, at the same time, still saw to my family's needs.

Occasionally, Mamma was placed in a nursing home for a week or so in order to give my father a rest. One such time when she was away, I visited Dad after work one Friday afternoon. I had decided to clean Mamma's bedroom. Before going up the stairs, I left Dad with instructions to make a 'nice cup of tea' in about half an hour.

On reaching the landing, I was brought to a sudden standstill by a dreadful feeling of fear swamping over me. A cold, familiar sensation of my hair standing on its ends ran along my scalp and my skin, causing me to shiver. The landing appeared darker than usual, although daylight was getting through from the open doors of a bedroom and the bathroom. My eyes searched the length of the gloomy landing and were drawn to a movement through the bannister of the attic stairs. I remained still and focused my eyes on the spot. I saw what I can only describe as a terrible blackness – just thick, deep, and very black, and in its hideous depth, all my senses told me that something was staring intensely out at me. At that moment, I knew that some damnable fiend still possessed the house. Wildly unnerved, I shot back down the stairs as fast as I could.

Two of the four photographs
taken of Mamma which
appear to show a white shape
in front of her: the shape
is dispersing on these, but
can still be seen. The first
two photographs have gone
missing.

Dad looked at me in puzzlement when I suddenly reappeared into the kitchen. 'I've changed my mind,' I said calmly, although I was shaking. 'I'll have the tea first, then do the bedroom later.' I walked over to the sink and filled the kettle, trying my best to make everything look as normal as possible.

'I need to sit down first,' I fibbed. 'I've been busy at work this morning.' His reply was a small nod and a smile indicating that he understood. Then he took over the preparation of making the tea. I wasn't sure if he was suspicious of my behaviour or not, but I felt as if he was. All the same, I didn't mention anything to him about what I had just felt and seen.

An hour or so passed before I went back up the stairs. Very cautiously, I approached the landing, not knowing what to expect. Thankfully, my caution was not needed: when I reached the top of the stairs, the landing had returned to normal. A shaft of sunlight shone out from one of the bedrooms and lit up the landing. I could see clearly along it. The sun's rays tapered through the bannister of the attic stairwell, displaying the patterned wallpaper decorating the wall of the stairs. This time I had an unobstructed view up the stairs. The black thing had gone!

One day at work, I overheard a conversation that two of my colleagues were having on the subject of ghosts. One girl said to the other that she would be really afraid if she saw a ghost walk by. I had no part in the conversation, but found myself interrupting them regardless. Without thinking, I asked them, 'But how would you know it was a ghost? It could just look like a stranger walking by, you know.'

'Because it would be see-through,' answered one of the girls.

'But they can be as solid as you and me,' I told her.

'Why; have you seen one?' asked the other.

I'd put my foot in it now. I looked around and realized that the conversation had taken the interest of everyone within earshot. All eyes were on me, waiting for my answer. I was annoyed that I had left myself so wide open: I'd never discussed the ghosts with anyone other than my family and the odd friend before, and that was only because they were already in the know. 'Yes, I have,' I answered truthfully.

Everyone's attention was still focused on me, waiting for my story. I didn't want to tell them anything, especially such a large audience. But I briefly told them of one or two incidents that had happened in the second house. I was amazed to find how interested they all were in what I'd said. All the same, I remained cautious in how much information I gave away because I knew only too well that someone would be bound to ridicule me. But to my surprise, no one did.

That night I could hardly sleep a wink. I was afraid that by my talking to everyone about the ghost, it would encourage it to come to my house. It was something I did not want to dabble with, and I didn't like to be reminded of it. To my relief, my fears were unfounded: nothing happened.

Slowly, over time, I found I was able to talk about the ghosts in more detail. My fear became an interest. My interest became an education. Having learned over the years to accept their existence, I also learned to appreciate my experiences, and the strange privilege of peeking into the other world, even if it was often scary. Unfortunately, coming to terms with the ghosts couldn't ward off other problems arising from the house.

In the late summer of 1982, my father was helping my mother down the steep stairs when they both fell. As a result, Mamma's leg was badly broken near the hip, which meant she spent many long months in hospital. It was clear that my father could no longer manage to take care of her. His own health and age had to be taken into consideration when we, the family, jointly made the decision to try and place Mamma in a home where she would be well looked after. This was no easy decision to make, and was even more difficult to have her accepted. Signatures had to be obtained from all kinds of different doctors and the like. Dad, Alfred, Edmond and I had to jointly sign an agreement before it could go ahead. It was a very sad day for all of us and we wished things had been different, but we all knew it was most definitely for the best. Except for a few days, Mamma was never to live in her own home again. Eventually, she settled happily in Oakwood Hall, Oakwood. It wasn't very far from Potternewton and she knew the area, so she could relate to her surroundings quite well.

Dad was now living alone, except for the company of the budgie and cat. Tony and I always made sure that we visited both my parents and his mother at least once a week, and that we were always on hand when needed. Our routine was to do our rounds every Sunday morning. Sometimes after I'd finished work early, I would call in to see my father. His health was not too good these days, so I kept a careful eye on him and did odd jobs around his house or ran errands.

Shortly after Mamma's move to Oakwood Hall, I went to the house in Potternewton to clear out her bedroom of old clothes and things that she no longer needed. When I arrived at the house, Dad seemed to be a little reluctant to let me go upstairs to her old room. He told not to bother clearing the room and to leave it for now, but I had purposely gone there to do it and I did not want a wasted journey. I couldn't understand why he had this attitude. It wasn't like him and I knew I was not intruding or anything, because I had already pre-arranged it with him.

I set off up the stairs regardless, with Dad following behind. With a slight air of haughtiness, I pushed open the door. The perverse disarray of furniture immediately struck me as I entered the room, and left me speechless. I glanced questioningly at my father, who had by now arrived at my side. We didn't speak, but silently took in the room. There was not the slightest bit of logic in the way that the furniture had been repositioned. It was like something out of a cartoon. The carpet was twisted into a spiral in the centre of the floor with one end of Mamma's single bed balanced on the top of it. The wardrobe was nearly in the corner of the opposite side of the room from its usual place, and was facing back to front. Everything was askew.

I looked at Dad, expecting an explanation from him. He answered with a weak smile and a shrug of his shoulders. He had an innocent expression on his face, and something about it told me not to make a fuss. If he was responsible for all this, for the life of me I could not understand why or how he could do it. Moving furniture was definitely out for him as he suffered from angina, and the change was pointless.

On vetting the room further, I found that things were even stranger than I first thought. All the soft fabrics in the room had rotted, except for the contents of one drawer. The curtains on the window, the carpet, clothes and even blankets folded neatly on the foot of the bed – all had rotted to the extent that they fell apart in my hands when I touched them.

Oakwood Hall, where Mamma lived, as it is today.

I had never seen anything like this in my entire life. Other rooms in the house had been empty for years, but nothing like this had ever happened to them. The house was admittedly old, but then, all the others in the street and surrounding areas were identical and of the same age. I'd never heard of any of the neighbours having the same or similar problems with their houses that my parents had with theirs. Previously, the backyard wall had been in danger of collapsing when it developed a large crack and began to lean. It was quickly repaired, no importance was placed on it, and it was accepted as being just one of those things. Similarly, the very large kitchen floor had become loose. Dad repeatedly reported it to the council. It was first noticed to be moving when the crockery in a cupboard and the cooker too began to rattle as one walked by. Eventually, the floor became worse. Even tip-toeing across the room caused everything in the cupboards to bounce. We used to laugh about it at first, but the house was getting beyond a joke, and I tried everything to persuade my father to leave it. But he was getting too old and ill to face all the upheaval.

Dad continued to report the floor to the council, but to no avail. Nobody ever came to look at it, let alone repair it. Then the time came when something had to be done. It had been three days since I last visited my father. I was surprised to see how much the floor had deteriorated in such a short time. It was now moving like a seesaw under my feet. Dad seemed to be oblivious to the danger as he sat in the middle of the room at the kitchen table. My presence did little to draw him away from a crossword puzzle that he was concentrating on. As I walked towards the table, a big sway from the floor startled me, causing me to cry out in alarm. At this, Dad at last looked up but just tut-tutted and said he was sick of reporting it.

I made my way down to the cellar to see if there had been changes to the ceiling below the kitchen. I could not see if the joists had collapsed, but noticed a small gap around the ceiling's edge. It wasn't like that before. I did not need to use any imagination to visualize the devastation that this huge ceiling and floor above would create if they were to fall. There was no homemade air-raid shelter in this house to use as a prop. I knew the whole thing was near to collapse, and was, ironically, ready to fall in the same manner as did the house of Grant Place. The odds of that happening once, let alone twice to the same family must have been very slim indeed. But here, staring me in the face, was the evidence that history was ready to repeat itself.

I ran up the steps from the cellar and immediately telephoned the council, telling them it was an emergency. I tried to explain to the clerk that if the floor was to push one of the surrounding walls as it fell, that it would bring the whole house down. I had great difficulty in getting him to understand the danger. He tried to fob me off, which made me angry. I told the clerk that I would have no choice but to call the emergency services, pointing out I'd let it be known that it was he who refused to help. Only then did he agree to send a maintenance man around. Now I understood why Dad had such a problem in trying to report it previously. I didn't care about the house, but I did care about my father's safety.

The same day, two workmen arrived with some props which looked as if they'd been taken from some old coalmine. One of the men went down into the cellar. He chipped away at the ceiling. Apparently, he found the whole thing quite amusing and laughed when he confirmed that the joists had gone. He went off to instruct the other fellow who was still sitting in the truck to unload the props, which he did. The first man then returned, carrying a prop under his arm, and trudged heavily across the kitchen floor. The floor gave a big heave with this extra weight, and lurched as if it were a ship at sea. 'Be careful,' I told him. With this he laughed at me, then deliberately caused the floor to rock some more, by dancing a little jig. 'Houses don't just fall down, you know,' he said in a patronising way, as if I was silly. He was the silly one, because I knew that they did. 'Oh, yes they do!' I answered sharply, 'His last one did.' I pointed to my father (who was still sitting at the table). Dad gave a weary nod to the man in agreement. I did not bother to waste my breath to explain anything to the workman, although he was now showing an interest in what I'd just said. The cellar looked dreadful with the props all over the place but they worked very well, and I could relax because I knew that Dad was now safe. No one ever came back to repair the floor correctly. I was not at all surprised at this because the council had once fitted a new sink unit into the kitchen, repositioning it, and never returned to take the old one out.

I tried again to talk my father into moving away, into a little bungalow or flat. This house was not only awful, but it was much too big for him. Also, the once smart Victorian area was rapidly going downhill. I could not coax him into leaving: he still refused to budge.

Ten

THE GHOSTS OF OAKWOOD HALL

It was a perfectly ordinary Sunday morning when Tony and I made our usual visit to Oakwood Hall to see my mother. We turned into the drive of the ivy-clad mansion, and, as always, my eyes quickly scoured the trees for squirrels as they darted away from our presence. We often saw their sweet little faces as they popped their heads around the branches of trees to take a peek at us, waiting for us to go inside so they could resume their play.

Even in a semi-neglected state, the was garden always lovely, with its big green lawn and magnificent trees. Mamma loved it. Weather permitting, she would sit under a tree for hours and enjoy the antics of the squirrels and birds. Today, though, it was too chilly to sit out. We guessed that she was most likely sitting in the Victorian conservatory as she often did. We sauntered through the front door and into the small but fairly grand hallway. A huge grandfather clock stood tidily in one corner and opposite this a staircase went up from one side of the hall and led to a landing, which resembled a gallery from the floor below. I knew that beyond the landing was a narrow passage. From there, another narrow flight of stairs led to Mamma's bedroom at the top of the house.

We could not see anyone in the staff's office, set back from a small corridor. We were just about to take it on ourselves to head for the Oak Room, which led onto the conservatory, when a young care assistant suddenly appeared from the dining room and called out to me.

'Are you Edna Slater's daughter?'

I answered with a nod as she headed towards us.

'Your mother gave me an awful fright the other night,' she blurted.

I nodded again, not because I understood, but just to signify that I was listening. But before I could ask her why, she told me anyway.

'We had a problem with staffing levels so I was on night shift on my own the other night. It was two o'clock in the morning, and I found her standing here.' She pointed to the staircase and wagged her finger at the third step up. 'I couldn't believe it. She was dressed properly; her hair was neatly brushed, and her shoes were fastened – you must know that she can't do all that by herself!'

The Oak Room at Oakwood Hall.

'Yes, I do know that.'

I expected the young woman to tell me that she made a mistake and that someone else had helped Mamma to dress and bring her down the stairs. It was extremely unlikely that Mamma had done this all alone, and impossible for her to tackle one flight of stairs on her own, let alone two. She could only walk with the help of a Zimmer frame, and would only do so when it was absolutely necessary; her normal routine was to use the lift.

I was shocked to think that only one person was on duty to look after thirty or so elderly people throughout the night. What if there had been a fire?

'Are you certain that you were the only person in the building that could have helped her?'

'Yes! But you won't believe me if I tell you what your mother said when I asked who had helped her.' She scrutinised my face, trying to predict my reaction.

'Try me!' I said, now intrigued.

'Who was it?' asked Tony as he moved in closer, not wanting to miss any of her answer.

'Well… I felt really scared when I saw her quietly standing there, because I knew there was just no way she could have got herself ready, and climbed down the stairs on her own. When I asked her what she was doing, she said a young girl, with long, dark hair brought her downstairs. The girl had apparently told her to get up and she helped her to dress. I know it sounds silly, but I think she was talking about a ghost!' She then added, 'I took her back upstairs in the lift. Then I was afraid to go into your mother's room. It really gave me the creeps!'

We had never mentioned the problems that we'd had with the ghosts to anyone in the home. We did not enlighten this young woman either, but I did ask her if the building was haunted.

The hall of Oakwood Hall. It was at the bottom of these stairs that my mother was found at 2 a.m.

'I'm beginning to believe it is,' she replied with a slight quiver in her voice.

'Where is my mother?' I asked calmly,. 'I'll see what she's got to say about all this.'

Following the direction of her pointing finger, Tony and I walked towards the Oak Room (so called because of the wood panelling on the walls). We thanked her and went in. Mamma was sitting near the fireplace, alone. She called as soon as we walked through the door. 'Colette! Anthony!' She never called him Tony. Before we could say 'hello', she asked in earnest, 'Who's that girl that keeps coming to me? She's got long, dark hair down to here.' She made a gesture with her hand at the lower part of her back. 'She wears clothes like I used to when I was a girl.' Then she asked, 'How did she find me here?' We walked towards her and I sat in an empty armchair next to her. Tony remained standing.

'I don't know. You tell me! You're the one who's seen her,' I said playfully.

'She comes to see me a lot; and she told me that she will always look after me – but who is she, Colette?'

'I already told you that I don't know. The next time she comes to see you – ask her who she is!'

'I will,' she answered, unconvincingly.

This time, I could not blame drugs for her imagination playing her up because she was no longer taking them. I tried to take her 'seeing things' lightly, but found it impossible to explain to myself how she got down the stairs, fully dressed! From that day on, Mamma frequently mentioned the girl and described her as being old fashioned. She did not recognise her, and eventually gave her name as being Margaret.

Yorkshire EVENING POST Final

THURSDAY JULY 31 1986 | TEL. LEEDS 432701 — Classified Advertising 441234 | **WEATHER PAGE 2** | PRICE 18p

THE GHOST of Oakwood Hall . . .

Oakwood Hall old people's home Oakwood, Leeds.

By NICOLA GOULD

Fire Brigade and council chiefs are baffled by a mystery burning smell which keeps returning in Oakwood Hall, a stately ivy-clad old people's home in Leeds.

After evacuating people from the old hall, and literally ripping it apart to check on the wiring and heating the mystery remained unsolved.

And when heat-seeking equipment used by the Fire Brigade last night also failed to pick up anything, Sub-Officer Norman Field, of Gipton, told the Yorkshire Evening Post:

"We will have to put it down to the ghost of Oakwood Hall."

The saga began on Saturday when staff at the council run home in Oakwood Grange Lane, smelt burning in the downstairs lounge, known as the Oak Room because of its wood panelling.

The brigade was called, but when they could find nothing to account for the smell, social services chiefs decided to evacuate the 38 elderly people from the building and put them

up in other homes in the city.

Mr. Keith Murray, assistant director of social services, said: "Over the weekend and on Monday we literally ripped the place apart. We took up floorboards and removed wood panelling to check the wiring. We looked at light fitting, and engineers checked the heating, but there was nothing amiss."

On Tuesday a meeting of fire service, social services and public works officers decided it was safe to allow the residents to return. But that wasn't the end of the story.

"Last night the burning

smell returned and the staff called the fire brigade again," Mr. Murray said.

Sub officer Field said: "We have been called to the Hall several times and last night we took thermal — imaging cameras to detect heat, but this showed nothing.

"We even swept the chimneys although they hadn't been used for years and got up on the roof to see if we could find anything.

Oakwood Hall is the former home of Sir Granville Gibson, Conservative MP for Pudsey and Otley from 1929 to 1945.

The Yorkshire Evening Post article.

As time passed, other reports of spooky incidents at Oakwood Hall were mentioned here and there by the staff but not necessarily involving my mother. A dramatic incident took place in the early morning of 28 July 1986 when all the residents including Mamma had to be evacuated from the building. (Thank God they had a full staff working at the time.) I received a telephone call from the home manager telling me that my mother had to be temporarily moved to another home because a cloud of smoke and a smell of burning were coming from the Oak Room. Tony and I went straight to her. We found her very distressed at being uprooted so suddenly and placed in strange surroundings, wearing only a nightdress, cardigan and just one slipper. She had no other clothes with her. We thought it best to take her home to our house, until she could return to Oakwood Hall.

We called into the hall on our way home while the fire fighters were still at the scene. We were told by a staff member that the smoke was seen to fill the room, which appeared to come up from the cellar, but nothing could be found to account for it down there. The mystery burning smell kept returning to the room, which baffled everyone including the fire brigade and the council chiefs.

The old mansion was literally ripped apart to check the wiring and the heating system but nothing was found to account for it. Heat-seeking equipment also failed to find anything. Before the thirty-eight elderly residents were returned to the house three days later, almost every inch of it had been scrutinised, including the chimneys and roof, but to no avail.

The day after everyone returned, the burning smell started again. Thermal imaging cameras used by the fire brigade again failed to detect anything amiss. They had to return to the mansion several times thereafter as the problem repeated itself – still nothing could be found. The local fire officer could only put it down to the ghost of Oakwood Hall!

I asked the home manager if these strange things going on started before, or after my mother went to live there. She thought for a moment, then said, 'They started after…!'

Eleven

DAD

In the meantime, strange things were still occurring back at the house in Potternewton. One afternoon, Dad went upstairs and found a light bulb sitting on the landing floor, outside the closed bathroom door. He was puzzled by it and wondered how it had got there. It had not fallen from the landing light fitting overhead. He picked it up and put it away.

Later that evening, he discovered that the light bulb had belonged in the bathroom because it was missing from the socket. He fetched his stepladder to put it back. The ceiling was very high, and as the bulb must have somehow fallen from its holder, he expected it to be broken. However, he tried it anyway. To his amazement it worked perfectly! But this did not answer the question as to how it found its way onto the landing through a closed door.

The children and I went to visit him one morning. We went into the house and found him in the sitting room crouched on his hands and knees. He was searching underneath the sideboard. For a moment, I thought he must have been looking for his cat, Tommy, until I heard his mew coming from the kitchen as he raced to greet us.

'What are you doing down there, Dad?' I startled him. He looked up in surprise; he had not released that we were there.

'I can't understand it,' he said as he got up from the carpet, scratching his bald head. 'I was sitting on the floor last night, watching television. You know how I like to sit with my legs stretched out with my back against the armchair,' he explained.

'Yes, I do.' I did know he liked to sit like that to relax. He found it comfortable, and I could just picture him.

'Well, for some reason, my watch started to hurt my wrist. So I took it off, and just popped it on the carpet – just there, next to the armchair.' He pointed to the exact spot before continuing. 'About an hour later, I reached out for the watch to see if it was time for the ten o'clock news on BBC, but it had gone!'

'Did you search underneath the chair? It might have got caught up on something.'

'I've looked everywhere, even in the kitchen just in case I took it in there, then forgot.

Dad in the backyard of his house in Potternewton.

But I know I didn't move from the spot. I hadn't even made myself a cup of tea, and I wanted one,' he said with his voice becoming exasperated.

'We'll help you to look,' I offered. 'Come on kids, you help too.'

We searched the entire room. We pulled furniture away from the wall, tipped up chairs to see if it was caught underneath, but the watch was nowhere to be seen. We even searched the kitchen, bathroom and his bedroom. Nothing was found.

Over the next few days, we continued the search, as did other visiting members of the family. I had vacuumed the carpet in the sitting room at least three times during this period. The watch was simply not there. By this time we had all stopped searching because it was pointless.

Two weeks later, I went to my father's house after I'd got an early finish from work. When I arrived, I found him all excited because he had found his watch, that very day.

'Where was it?' I asked with great interest.

'You're not going to believe it, but I went into the sitting room to watch the lunch-time news on television and as soon as I opened the door, I saw it – on the floor next to the armchair, exactly in the same spot where I'd first left it!'

It was early evening, Christmas day 1986 and at my house my parents, Tony, and his widowed mother, Mrs Shires, were waking up one by one after snoozing in the comfortable armchairs; the large Christmas dinner we'd eaten had had a soporific effect on them. Julia and I were just happy to be able to settle and watch television after washing a mountain of dishes. Alan was in his bedroom, reading. This was more or less the usual Christmas day scene in our house since Mamma's accident.

Tony, Alan and Julia on the
back steps of Dad's house in
Potternewton.

It was well after seven o'clock before we'd had tea and came back to life. Tony was expecting to drive my parents and his mother home later. He wanted to do this in one trip, so he asked his mother if she would leave around nine o'clock when he planned to take Mamma back to Oakwood Hall. While this was being discussed between them, Julia assumed that her Granddad was going to stay the night at our house because she didn't hear his name mentioned.

'Don't you want to go back to your haunted house, Granddad?' She asked him bluntly.

'What do you mean my haunted house?' he answered her with a question and gave a nervous laugh. 'My house is not haunted.' He usually scorned the idea of ghosts as soon as they were mentioned, even though he had complained only days before of a heavy weight pinning him down on his bed. Others who had stayed at the house in the past also experienced the same thing. In spite of everything that had happened, he still would not acknowledge that the house was not normal.

'Mrs Shires, did you know that our house fell down?' piped in my mother as some vague memory drifted back to her.

'Yes, I did! That was strange, wasn't it? But what is Julia talking about ghosts for?' she asked in a puzzled tone.

'Yes, what are you talking about ghosts for, Julia?' chuckled my father.

'Oh! Granddad, you know that the house is haunted,' she said. 'I remember going down in your cellar when I was around seven or eight years old. I'd gone to fetch a bottle of your home brew for my dad,' she recalled. 'When I got down there, I suddenly felt really scared, but I didn't know why. I grabbed the bottle, and turned to run back up when I saw a black-sleeved arm wrap around the wall at the bottom of the steps. I screamed and yelled until my dad came to me and took me back up to the kitchen. I told everybody about it at the time, but nobody would believe me because I was a child.' She looked at my father's smiling face, then retorted, 'Even now that I'm sixteen and older, still, nobody will listen to me!' Exasperated by the lack of response, she flopped back into her chair and blew out her cheeks.

We were all listening to her, and everyone's eyes turned swiftly from her to my father, waiting in anticipation for his reaction to all this. His response was just to continue chuckling. I had waited long enough for him to admit that this second house was also haunted, so now that the subject had been raised, I cheekily challenged him to give logical explanations to account for all the strange things that had happened over the years. I gave it little thought that Mamma, and my mother-in-law, who I'd never mentioned the ghosts to, were listening. Mrs Shires, never having heard the likes of all this before, said nothing, but sat there with her eyes and mouth wide in amazement at what she was hearing.

'Come on, Dad. Have you ever heard of any other family having to put up with all these things? You've got to confess that things are not right in your house, just as they were not right in Grant Place!'

'Colette!' he snapped. 'You have forgotten something!'

'What have I forgotten?' I asked tauntingly.

'I have to live there on my own!' His words pressed towards me. I hadn't thought about that. And the instant he spoke, his eyes told me that he did accept that the house had problems, and his reluctance to admit it was his way, as it was once mine, to cope with it. I felt ashamed of my goading him, and did not discuss it any further and the subject was quickly changed.

It was not to be known then that this was to be our last Christmas with Dad and Tony's mother; they both died the following year. It was only three months later, in March 1987, at the age of seventy-two, that Mrs Shires passed away from cancer; Dad's turn came in November 1987. He was aged seventy-six. He too died of cancer, but not before he had an accident after a night out with his pals in the August. He was fun-loving and very much enjoyed his leisure time. He looked much younger than his age, but a game of dominoes and three or four pints of his favourite beer was about as much 'living it up' that he could handle by then.

The accident happened just after he'd left the Victoria pub in the Sheepscar area of Leeds, just before closing time. He was crossing the road and heading for his bus stop when a police car swiftly appeared around a bend, heading towards him. He was almost across the road, but as his legs were not too good, he couldn't move quickly enough to get out of its path. The car hit him sideways-on. The police were responding to a call regarding a stolen car and were hoping to head it off further up the road. Unfortunately, Dad was in the wrong place at the wrong time. Apart from being very shaken, a grazed and twisted foot appeared to be his worst injury, but it marked the beginning of the end for him. His health went downhill from that time and he died twelve weeks later.

Before he went to hospital I took care of him at my house. Twice a day, Tony called at Dad's house to tend to Tommy (we were unable to bring Tommy to our home because Alan is allergic to cats; Peter, the budgie, had died a few month's before).

He was never quite sure if he should believe in ghosts or not. Although he did find the house in Potternewton to be just as spooky as the house in Grant Place, he lacked the experience of coming across a ghost in either of them, so he could not make up his mind – until he encountered something in the second house that frightened him and for which he could find no rational explanation.

He first noticed something was wrong when he sat in the kitchen with Tommy after feeding him. For no apparent reason, the doors leading to the hall and cellar simultaneously slammed shut. This, of course, unnerved him, and more so when he couldn't find an explanation; it wasn't windy or anything. This small incident gave him a hint that the stories he'd heard over the years just might be true. But it took a further, much more frightening incident to convince him.

This happened when, as usual, he called into the house on his way home from work. It was November, and the long, dark winter nights had well and truly set in. On his return home, even before eating, he explained to me what happened when he unlocked the front door of my father's house, which opened into a long, narrow hallway. The door to the kitchen was at the far end; to the left was the door to the front room and between them was the stairs to the bedrooms and the light switches.

'As soon as I opened the door, I heard a noise coming from inside,' he said. 'With the help of the streetlights outside, I could just see down the dim hall, but not clearly enough to see what I'd startled at the foot of the stairs as I went in. I was terrified to hear something as big as a man noisily scurry up the stairs as it fled. The first thought in my mind was a burglar. My skin crawled as if I was cold, then I felt as if my hair on my head was standing up.'

'What did you do then?' I asked, intrigued and worried.

'I immediately shot down the hall and switched on a light, then looked up the stairs – but saw nothing.'

'Could it have been Tommy?'

'No! The first thing I did was look around for him. I found him sitting in the kitchen, waiting for me. Besides, the noise I heard could not have come from him, because a cat is too small and silent on its paws. The 'thing' on the stairs was much too big and heavy to have been Tommy.'

I bombarded him with questions: Tony said he had checked to see if the house had been burgled, but everything was fine. He told me that he did not mind admitting that he was afraid, so he opened the front and back doors as wide as he could, just as a precaution on the off chance that he might have to flee the house. (I recalled doing a similar thing myself when I was afraid in the house.) Tommy was fed and tended to at high speed so he could leave quickly. Tony could not bring himself to walk back through the house the same way he came in, so he left instead through the back door, locking it behind him. He then walked up the street and around the block to the front door, which he then locked and went home. From that day, Tony was convinced that the house was indeed haunted.

We were very distressed to learn that my father had cancer, which had spread throughout his body, and his chances of surviving much longer were nil. He took the news from his doctors with great strength. I was proud of his courage, but it took a massive heart attack to finish him off in the end. He passed away peacefully, and with dignity, in the small hours.

Julia, Alan, me and Tony in Dad's front room in Potternewton. Note the china cabinet on the right – a suspected ghost carrier.

On clearing out his house, I was too afraid to take anything from it in the shape of a container or vessel that could have harboured a ghost, no matter of its size. I was sure that ghosts could be carried from one house to another in such an object. Apart from a few family documents and family photographs, I took very little. No one else in the family would take anything either, with the exception of Alfred. He was the only one to take a risk and he took some of the larger items. One of them was being the china cabinet, which remarkably had survived the collapse of the first house. Everything else was either sold for a pittance to strangers or dumped. I often wonder if any of these unsuspecting people had inherited any of the ghosts.

We had great difficulty in finding a new home for Tommy. Eventually, when we did (through a cat rescue society) it was discovered that he had cancer, and had to be put down. It seemed strange and so sad, that my father and both of his pets had died in such a short space of time.

The house in Potternewton still stands, and all contact with it has been severed. I don't know if any of the ghosts are still present there, or who lives in the house now. The area has since become very grim and I have no reason to visit it. Sometimes, though, I wish I had the nerve to go there and knock on the door and ask out of curiosity. But I'm sure the new occupiers, whoever they are, would not take kindly to me doing that.

Two years after my father's death, Mamma reached her eightieth birthday. Tony and I always tried to improve her life the best we could. I always felt so sad for her. I didn't expect many people to come to the birthday party I'd planned for her because she hadn't seen most of her old friends for years, and some had died. By this time the only living relatives and in-laws she had left from her generation were her brothers Tigue, who lived in Leeds, and Freddie and his wife Betty in Australia, and her sister-in-law, Mary, in Ireland. So it was wonderful news when I received a letter from Mary telling me that she was coming over to Leeds with three of her children and my brother Conrad for the party. Mamma was very fond of Mary, and wept when she saw her, which in turn made everyone else cry. Mary made her party special and it warmed my heart.

Twelve

THE HOLLIES

Mamma asked Tony if he would take her on a trip, 'to sit on the top of a big hill so I can see for miles and miles.'

'Aw, Edna. We'll never find a hill big enough to take your weight,' he teased. She shrieked with laughter at his jibe.

'What about yourself?' she quipped. His face took on a pretend look of shock at her remark, which he quickly turned to an affectionate grin. She smiled up at him with a child-like innocence, making us aware once again of the compassion we both felt for her.

'Of course I'll take you,' he said gently, and gave her hand a small squeeze. Then with a start, he straightened up as if he'd been stung.

'What do you want to go up a hill for? I hope you're not thinking of jumping off!'

Mamma instantly burst into laughter again, her face vibrant with life. I smiled to see her like this, and especially displaying her untarnished sense of humour, which was still very active. She had been told that Oakwood Hall was to close down and she was to be moved to The Hollies. Many elderly people's homes were closing at the time, and Oakwood Hall was no exception, even though it had been the home for many people, including my mother, for years. The move held many fears for her – including some that the other residents did not have to consider.

'What about Margaret? How will she know where I am?' she asked.

As we drove home that day, the wind was still tinged with wintry ice, and the thought of being up any hill on a cold March day sent a shudder down my back. As we drove, we talked about her question. 'What about Margaret, the ghost? Real or imaginary, she has been good for my mother – hasn't she? But I can't think of anything that we can do about her! And I really don't want to put any ideas into Mamma's head about ghosts, so I can't suggest anything to her.' Tony didn't speak, but simply nodded. I knew without asking that he too could not come up with any suggestions. Silently, we continued our drive home.

In the end we decided it was best not to mention a word about 'Margaret' to my mother, and hoped she would forget about her. Alfred agreed to say nothing as well. The chances were high that she would forget, because her memory was very bad since her accident.

Mamma in the Oak Room at Oakwood Hall.

Mamma had an uncomplicated transfer to The Hollies in 1991. The residents and the staff made her feel so welcome that when the day arrived for her to move in, she was quite happy about it. After that, every effort was made to help settle her in. As soon as she was settled, she surprised us by remembering our promise to take her up a big hill. We had no intentions of letting her down, so her trip was soon arranged.

The sun had been shining since the early morning, and it promised to be a perfect day. To Mamma's delight, we took her to the beautiful Yorkshire Dales, and found the perfect hill. Parking was a little difficult on the hill because of unlevelled ground, but we managed to find a small flat area just big enough to fit the car on, at the edge of the road. To reach the brow of the hill meant a short walk for an able-bodied person, but it was a long and difficult walk for my mother, even with help. Tony, and Alfred's wife, Sheila, who was with us, almost had to carry Mamma across the uneven turf. I trundled along ahead, loaded up with flasks for a cuppa, and blankets for us to sit on. Our efforts were worth it.

We found a spot with the best possible view of a deep valley below. It funnelled out at one end, to meet a wide-open space, which gently ascended at the far side to mountainous hills, and huddled in the centre of the flat land below them, the tiny houses and buildings of Ainscliffe could be seen. Opposite, on the other side of the valley, another huge hill about the same size as the one we were on exposed its limestone body. The lush grass growing on its top gave the impression it was wearing a large green wig with a short stubby fringe.

Mamma happy on the hill in the Yorkshire Dales.

'It's so beautiful,' cried Mamma as her eyes drew in the sights, and filled her face with contentment. We sat quietly relaxing in the sun, and sank into our own thoughts. My thoughts drifted toward my mother, and how she had remembered our promise. We had a lovely day out. The weather stayed in our favour so we travelled around a while after leaving the big hill and had a picnic next to a stream. Mamma loved the whole trip and did not want it to end.

Mamma had not mentioned one word about Margaret the ghost in her new home. I guessed that she must have forgotten about her by now, and I didn't expect to hear anything about her or any ghost again – but I was wrong. Five months or so had gone by after our visit to the Dales, when Margaret made her appearance to Mamma again. This news took us by surprise, especially after all this time, and in a different place.

It was almost Christmas; Tony and I had been invited to a party at The Hollies. This house was also a large old mansion, similar to Oakwood Hall, only this time the garden was very well kept, and was tended to by a local botanist. And like Oakwood Hall, there were plenty of trees, squirrels, and birds to keep my mother's interest in life going. She spent most of her days as she did at Oakwood Hall, sitting in a small conservatory, which looked out over the drive and garden. Alfred lived in Meanwood, not very far away, so he visited her more often now and called in to see her while taking his dog for a walk in Meanwood Park. Sometimes he took her around the park in a wheelchair. She was happy, which, in turn, made me happy.

The front of The Hollies.

When we arrived for the party, we expected my mother to be with the rest of the residents, enjoying the celebrations, but she wasn't. She wanted to go into a sitting room well away from all the activity. A lady who, I would estimate, was well into her nineties was sleeping in a chair in a corner of the room. Mamma looked at her from top to bottom, before turning her attention to a frail old gentleman sitting at the far side of the room, engrossed in watching television. After satisfying herself that these other two occupants of the room were not taking the slightest heed that we were there, Mamma crooked her finger, and beckoned for us to listen to her. Tony put his ear to her mouth, thinking she was going to whisper something. Instead, she surprised us both by suddenly yelling in excitement:

'She found me... Margaret has found me – here!' She tugged at my jacket sleeve as if I wasn't listening. 'Did you tell her where I was?' she asked.

'No! How could I tell her? I've never even seen her,' I laughed, then added, 'are you sure it was her you saw, and not just a visitor or someone?'

'Of course I'm sure it was her.' She stiffened up her body and continued. 'She told me that she would always find me, no matter where I went, and that she would always take care of me!' Mamma tugged at my sleeve again, making sure she had all my attention; she pulled me towards her. 'Colette, I told her that she'd got a bit older since I'd last saw her, and she laughed when I said that.'

'How old is she?' I asked.

Another view of The Hollies.

'She did tell me, but I forgot what she said. I think she's about eighteen now.'

Tony and I looked across at each other. Neither of us knew what to make of this latest news.

'Has anyone else seen her?' I asked.

'I don't know – but she really does come, Colette!' She said it as if I doubted her. Mamma let her hand drop from my sleeve, then added, 'She wears old-fashioned clothes. The last time I saw her she was wearing a costume. Another time, she wore some trews.' That was the first time since the 1960s that I'd heard a woman's two-piece suit being called a costume, I'd almost forgotten that's what they were called then, and I must have been a child since I last heard of women's trousers being referred to as trews.

Mamma shuffled around in her chair like she often did, then said, almost to herself this time, 'The clothes she wore before were like the ones I used to wear when I was a young girl.' Mamma was more informative this time, and was able to give more details about Margaret's clothes than usual. From her descriptions, I conjured up a picture in my mind of the ghost being dressed in the fashion of the 1920s or '30s.

'When you see her again, ask as many questions as you can – try your best to remember what she says and find out who she is!' Again, I asked her to do this as I frequently did in the past, but her memory usually let her down, but on occasions, like now, her memory was very clear.

I was very curious about this 'Margaret' story, and was completely baffled with the getting older bit. I had tried to get to the bottom of it by asking the staff at Oakwood Hall, and now the staff at The Hollies, if my mother had received any visitors of Margaret's description. I never told them why I was asking these questions, but I always drew a blank.

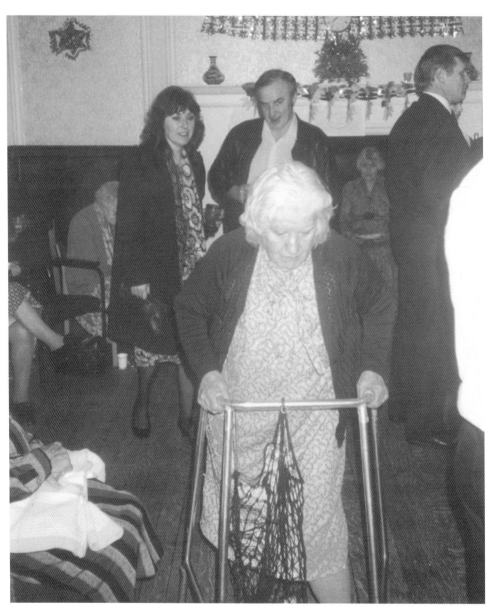

Mamma as a party pooper in The Hollies when she wanted to tell us about her ghost finding her. (Tony and I are behind her.)

Tony and I were pretty good at determining what was what with Mamma when she was confused. We could often unravel things by asking her lots of questions. On the subject of Margaret however, she never once faulted, and was always most definite about her appearances. We could never forget the incident with Mamma on the stairs of Oakwood Hall so we kept a very open mind. Although Mamma began to see Margaret quite often at The Hollies, we were never able to establish who she was.

Thirteen

THE CROFT

A few short months later, it was announced that The Hollies was to close as well. As we expected, the move caused Mamma a great deal of distress. Her new home was on the other side of Leeds, in Seacroft. The building was modern; we knew she would find this difficult to relate to, as she would the surrounding area. She never had any connections with Seacroft before, and it was very different from anywhere she had lived in the past. There were no trees or squirrels for her to watch and no real garden for her to sit in. To make matters even worse, she was allocated to the top floor, which distressed her even further. She could not relate to any of this. The change was too much for her, and all was not well. Alfred's visits had to be cut down by more than half as it now took two bus journeys for him to reach The Croft.

Mamma's room was simple but nice, and she had it to herself. The staff took care of her, though my mother did not get on with them quite as well as the staff in the previous homes. However, there was another issue that was bothering her quite apart from all these changes. During one of our visits, Mamma tearfully asked Tony and I, 'Why doesn't Margaret come to me anymore? I'll bet she can't find me here. She won't know where I am!' We had no way of answering that question. I wished Margaret would turn up, ghost or not.

More than a year and a half later, our wish was granted. Margaret had arrived at last. We were delighted to hear of this from Mamma. Whatever or whoever Margaret was did not matter, because she made my mother happy. I could quite easily have developed affection for this ghost, as silly as it seems. She seemed to be the only one that could bring peace to the whole tragic saga of my mother's life since her accident.

The time came when it was no longer very difficult to believe that Margaret was a ghost. Another resident, whom I'd never spoken to before, fully backed up my mother's story when she overheard Mamma telling Tony and I about Margaret's latest visit as we walked her from her room to the lounge.

'She's right, you know,' a voice spoke out from behind us, taking us by surprise.

'Yes, she'll tell you,' Mamma said excitedly, and pointed to a woman sitting nearby in the dining area.

'She's telling the truth,' the lady responded without hesitation, and most passionately, she added, 'I've seen the pair of them together – they were both coming out of her room. But the girl, she didn't come in here!'

'Really, you really saw her?' I asked in amazement.

'Yes, she does come to her – I've seen her,' she repeated, and went on to give the same description of Margaret as my mother had. She seemed sensible enough, a sort of school teacher type, I thought. I had no reason to doubt what she had said. So there we were, with more evidence of Margaret's existence.

A few weeks later, just as I was preparing to leave for work, the telephone rang.

'Mrs Shires?'

'Yes?'

'This is the matron from The Croft. Your mother's not well and she's been taken to Seacroft Hospital.'

I'd had a number of these calls in the past for various reasons, and I was not unduly worried because she was tough and things usually turned out not to be very serious.

'Is it bad, or is it just another one of her diabetic dos?' I asked.

'I don't know, but I think you should go there, she's not good.'

'Okay. I'll go. Thank you.' As I replaced the receiver, something about this call made me feel uneasy. Before I left for the hospital, I first rang Alfred to let him know. Then I rang Julia and asked her to ring my boss a little later as it was too early then. She also telephoned Tony and Alan, who were working together.

I arrived at the hospital and found the ward.

'Excuse me!' I said to a passing nurse, 'I'm looking for Edna Slater; she was brought here this morning. Could you tell me where she is, please? I'm her daughter.'

'Oh! Yes, err. She's down here,' she said, and led the way down a long corridor. I followed quickly in her footsteps.

'How is she?' I asked.

The nurse stopped and turned towards me. 'She's… she's dead,' she answered gently. Her words hit me like a sledge hammer. 'We did everything we could to resuscitate her, but it was too late. We think she was already D.O.A… didn't you know?'

I had already stopped in my tracks. My eyes exploded into tears. Yes, I did know – something deep inside me told me the news was going to be bad. I did not want to hear it. I was not at all ready for it. The worst of all was that she'd gone before I got here – it was all over, and I was not with her.

The nurse took me to the small room where Mamma lay on a bed. I was surprised to see everyone had already got there before me. They were sitting very quietly with tear-filled eyes. Mamma was laid on the bed, still in her nightgown. I knew then that she must have taken ill as soon as she got up. I felt through the blankets for her hand and found a clenched fist, and held it. I could see that she was gone – really gone. She'd had a massive heart attack. She was aged eighty-four.

In all, I am comforted in knowing that she was never afraid of dying, and accepted the idea of death with ease, unlike anyone else I'd ever known. All she ever wanted was to be

Me at the time of writing.

with her mother and father again. She often asked me with impatience, 'When will I kick the bucket, Colette?' I was glad that she had Margaret as a friend, and hoped that she'd been around that inevitable morning.

I cannot say that the story ends here, because it is not so. The ghosts still linger in the shadows of our time, and their world entwines with ours. They have not gone: they have changed their course only. In the past they have proven to be able to do so, perhaps caused by some unintentional intervention, like carrying them from place to place in furniture or objects which are able to contain them. Or perhaps they chose their own destination and wanted to follow my family. Who knows? Perhaps one or two of the ghosts from my parents' houses could have latched onto someone else's family. They may have items of furniture originating from the Potternewton house in their home, as has my brother Alfred – reports of ghostly activities have taken place in his house. The ghosts have moved, and a new story has begun!

The End...

Other titles published by The History Press

Paranormal West Yorkshire

ANDY OWENS

This richly illustrated book covers a fascinating range of strange events, from famous cases such as the Cottingley Fairies – a mystery which puzzled countless investigators (including Sir Arthur Conan Doyle) – to UFO sightings and hauntings in West Yorkshire's pubs, manor houses and private residences.

978 07524 4810 7

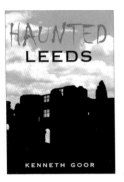

Haunted Leeds

KENNETH GOOR

From creepy accounts of the city centre and surrounding suburbs to phantoms of the theatre, haunted hotels and pubs, *Haunted Leeds* contains a chilling range of ghostly goings-on. Drawing on historical and contemporary sources, you will hear about the ex-librarian who haunts Leeds Library, the ghost of a murderer at the Town Hall, Mary Bateman the Leeds Witch, as well as many other spectral monks, soldiers and white ladies!

978 07524 4016 3

South Shields Poltergeist

MICHAEL J. HALLOWELL & DARREN RITSON

Here is a chilling diary of an ongoing poltergeist case which rivals any previously documented. In December 2005, a family began to experience typical but low-level poltergeist-like phenomena in their home. Slowly but steadily the phenomena escalated: knives, coins and other objects began to be thrown, mysterious messages appeared on a child's 'doodle board' – and then the spirit began to attack the authors...

978 07509 4874 6

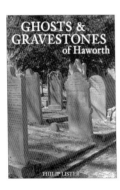

Ghosts & Gravestones of Haworth

PHILIP LISTER

Join local guide Philip Lister as he takes you on a tour of Haworth's dark and ghostly side: meet the ghost of Room 7 at the Old White Lion Hotel, the Grey Lady of Weavers Restaurant, and Ponden Hall's harbinger of doom, Old Greybeard. Tour the famous graveyard, in use for over 700 years and believed to house over 40,000 souls.

978 07524 3958 8

If you are interested in purchasing other books published by The History Press, or in case you have difficulty finding any History Press books in your local bookshop, you can also place orders directly through our website
www.thehistorypress.co.uk

Ultimate Buyers'

Land Rover Discovery (1989-1998)

and Discovery Series II (1998-2004)

James Taylor
PMM Books

First published 2005

ISBN 09545579 7 2

Published by PMM Books, an imprint of Peter Morgan Media Ltd.,
PO Box 2561, Marlborough, Wiltshire, SN8 1YD.
Telephone: +44 1672 514038
E-mail: sales@pmmbooks.com
Website: www.pmmbooks.com

Land Rover Discovery (1989-1998) and Discovery Series II (1998-2004)
Contents

Introduction	5
Timeline for Discovery and Discovery Series II	6
Facts, figures and performance for Discovery and Discovery Series II	12
Discovery background	17
Model changes year by year – Discovery I	
Chassis frame	21
Bodyshell	21
Equipment and accessories	22
Interior	23
Engine	24
Transmission	26
Suspension and steering	27
Brakes, wheels and tyres	27
Model designations	29
Model changes year by year – Discovery Series II	
Chassis frame	32
Bodyshell	32
Equipment and accessories	33
Interior	33
Engine	35
Transmission	36
Suspension and steering	37
Brakes, wheels and tyres	38
Model designations	40
Special models	
Discovery I	42
Discovery Series II	46
Production information	
Vehicle Identification Number information	49
Year by year body colours and interior choices	52
Options	58
Buying a used Discovery	
Discovery culture	58
Documentation	61
Chassis frame	62
Bodywork	62
Interior	64
Engines	66
Transmission	68
Suspension and steering	69
Brakes, wheels and tyres	70
About the author and Acknowledgements	72

Land Rover
Discovery I and II

Introduction

Land Rover's Discovery was a massive success for the company, swiftly becoming its best-seller and, in many countries, also a best-seller in its class. That means there are many thousands of examples now on the second-hand market, while the large number of different varieties built has led to a real need for the sort of purchasing help that this Ultimate Buyers' Guide aims to provide.

The Discovery name lives on, of course. In mid-2004, Land Rover announced the Discovery 3 (known as the LR3 in North America), and no doubt that will go on to become just as successful and well-respected as the two original models to bear the name. But it is a very different vehicle from the models dealt with in this book.

When the second-generation Discovery was announced in 1998, Land Rover badged it as the Series II model. That automatically led to the earlier models being known as Series I types, and I've used that terminology in this book. For what it's worth, though, the name "Series I" was never used when the vehicles were in current production.

Within both the Series I and Series II ranges, there are two subdivisions. The Series I models were heavily revised in March 1994, and among the key revisions was a change from the 200 Tdi to the 300 Tdi diesel engine. As diesel Discoverys predominated in most markets, this led many people to refer to the earlier models as the "200 series" and the later ones as the "300 series". Clearly, those names make no sense for petrol-engined Discoverys, and

are nonsensical in North America, where all Discoverys were V8s and all were sold after March 1994! Nevertheless, it's pointless to go against common practice, so you will find the names 200 series and 300 series used in this book, too.

As for the Series II models, their major facelift came in mid-2002 for the 2003 models. In fact, the 2003 and 2004 Discoverys weren't actually badged as Series II types at all. It's common practice to describe these later examples simply by their model-year ("2003 model" or "2004 model") and so I've done the same here.

The Discovery was sold in markets all around the world, and Land Rover used different permutations of equipment to create specifications which suited each market. Obviously, there isn't room in a book this size to record every different specification, so I've focussed on the two primary markets of the UK and North America.

All Discoverys are hugely practical vehicles, and they make an ideal purchase either as family transport or for the dual-purpose role of everyday driver plus weekend off-roader. Build quality problems, particularly in the mid-1990s, also gave them a rather bad reputation. So one of the aims of this guide is to help you avoid the real dogs and to buy a Discovery that you'll be able to use and enjoy for many years. Good hunting!

James Taylor, Oxfordshire, UK

Timeline for the Discovery Series I

This timeline (and the references used throughout the text) is based on the Land Rover model year, which normally runs from September to August. Thus, a 1990 model would have been built between September 1989 and August 1990.

1990
Discovery introduced in November 1989 as 3-door model with 111bhp (81kW) 2.5-litre 200 Tdi turbocharged diesel engine or 144bhp (106kW) 3.5-litre V8 carburettor petrol engine. All models have 5-speed LT77 manual gearbox and LT230T 2-speed transfer gearbox. 5-seat configuration standard; 7-seat configuration optional. All models have styled steel wheels with 205 R 16 tyres.

1991
5-door body introduced as alternative to 3-door. V8 engines fitted with fuel injection, increasing power to 164bhp (120kW); models so equipped are known as V8i types. Catalytic converter optional, reducing power to 153bhp (112kW). 5-spoke 16-inch alloy wheels introduced as line-build option for 5-door models.

1992
Gearbox receives improved synchromesh and is now known as LT77S type.

1993
4-speed automatic gearbox option introduced for V8i models only, using ZF 4HP22 gearbox. Commercial derivative added to range in April 1993.

1994
V8i models now equipped with 180bhp (132kW) 3.9-litre engine. Third engine option introduced: models with new 134bhp (98kW) 2.0-litre petrol engine are badged as Mpi types. Automatic option now extended to Tdi models. Front and rear anti-roll bars become optional, with Freestyle alloy wheels and 235/70 R 16 tyres.

1995
Facelifted models introduced in March 1994 as 1995 models. Discovery launched into North America with facelift specification as 5-door V8i model only. Side impact beams added to rear doors of North American Specification (NAS) Discoverys in summer

Discovery Series I

The earliest Discoverys were all three-doors and all had distinctive side graphics

With the facelifted models of the so-called "300 series" in 1994 came a new top model badged in the UK as the ES

1994.

Revised headlamps, grille and front apron; revised rear lights with turn indicators and fog guard lamps now in bumper; new alloy wheel designs. Restyled dashboard with provision for driver's and passenger's airbags. New heating and air conditioning (HVAC) system with separate driver's and passenger's side temperature controls. Height-adjustable steering wheel. Revised centre console, new door trims, and new interior fabrics. Leather standard on top models, 6-way power adjustment for front seats with leather trim.

More refined 300 Tdi turbodiesel engine replaces 200 Tdi type; power output unchanged. Small power increase for V8i engines, to 182bhp (133kW); catalytic converter now standard. Increased torque for Mpi four-cylinder petrol engines.

New R380 five-speed manual gearbox replaces LT77S type. Front brake discs now ventilated on all models; ABS standard on top models and optional on others. Anti-roll bars standardised front and rear. 235/70 tyres standard on top models.

1996

300 Tdi engines in automatic models now equipped with Electronic Diesel Control (EDC) and delivering 120bhp (88kW).

"4.0-litre" V8 engine replaces 3.9-litre type on NAS models; power and torque outputs unchanged. V8i types for other markets continue with 3.9-litre V8.

LT230Q transfer box replaces LT230T type on NAS models.

Half-leather upholstery introduced (on XS models in UK). 8-way power adjustment for ES front seats. Engine immobilser standardised; smaller remote-control handset for immobiliser alarm and central locking.

Bodystyle Choice bodykit option introduced in December 1996.

1998

Mpi engine discontinued. Centre high-mounted stop lamp standardised; new rear lamp clusters; headlamp levelling standardised. New alloy wheel designs.

Kestrel cloth interior trim replaces Gleneden. Rear centre armrest added to models with full- or half-leather trim. Walnut facia trim for top models. Premium Trim Pack of Lightstone leather becomes optional (accompanied by wing and tailgate badging).

Heated windscreen available for 5-door models only; electric front windows standard on all models.

1999

"Series I" Discovery no longer in production. Last few NAS models sold with SD badges and 1999 model-year VIN identification alongside first Series II models.

Timeline for the Discovery Series II

All North American Discovery II models had V8 petrol engines, but in other respects they differed from vehicles for other markets mainly in equipment levels. Important changes to the North American Discovery II models are noted below.

1999

Series II models introduced in November 1998, all with 5-door bodies. 5-seat configuration standard; 7-seat optional. Engines are 182bhp (133kW) 4.0-litre petrol V8 or 134bhp (98kW) 2.5-litre turbocharged and intercooled "Td5" 5-cylinder diesel. Choice of 5-speed R380 manual gearbox or ZF 4HP22 4-speed automatic, each driving through LT230SE 2-speed transfer gearbox. No central differential lock, but 4-wheel ETC standard, operating through the standard ABS system. Most models with ACE anti-roll control on front suspension; SLS height-adjustable air springs replace rear coil springs on some models. ATC heating, air conditioning and ventilating system available.144 Series II models built from knock-down kits in Malaysia.

2000

Compass in rear-view mirror of top models. From mid-way in 2000 MY, Duragrain PVC upholstery is introduced for entry-level models in North America only.

2001

Low-volume assembly from knock-down kits resumes at Volvo plant in Malaysia. Discovery Series II Commercial introduced to UK market in May 2001.

2002

All engines meet new EU3 emissions regulations. V8s restricted to mid-range and top models in the UK. Increased torque for Td5 automatics. New alloy wheel options; new premium Harmon-Kardon ICE systems and satellite navigation.

2003

Facelift with restyled headlamps and shallower front spoiler; driving lamps inset into bumper; restyled rear lamps now with turn indicators; reversing lights and fog lamps in bumper. Central differential lock available at extra cost. Revised suspension geometry, improved brakes, improved body mountings and noise insulation. Three new interior colours, black dash replaces grey. Styled "Aero" roof rails, Park Distance Control option and new alloy wheels introduced. North American models get 4.6-litre V8 engine as standard.

2004

Last Discovery Series II built in May 2004.

Discovery Series II

One easy way of recognising a Discovery II is by its flush-glazed rear windows and Alpine lights, and by the lower-mounted tail light clusters

Facts, figures and performance

Discovery Series I

Chassis

14-gauge steel ladder-frame type with box-section members, five cross-members and 10 rubber body mounts.

Bodyshell

Steel inner skeleton with steel roof and rear corner panels; other outer panels in aluminium alloy. 3-door or (from 1991 model year) 5-door configuration.

Engines

Diesel: 200 Tdi (1990-1994 models) or 300 Tdi (1995-1998 models) 4-cylinder with direct injection, turbocharger and intercooler. Iron block and alloy cylinder head; five main bearings; belt-driven camshaft. Bore 90.47mm, stroke 97mm, capacity 2495cc. Compression ratio 19.5:1. Maximum power 111bhp (83kW) at 4000 rpm; maximum torque 195 lb.ft (265Nm) at 1800 rpm.

On 1996-1998 models with automatic transmission, the 300 Tdi engine has EDC and delivers 120bhp (90kW) and 221lb.ft (300Nm) at the same crankshaft speeds.

Mpi petrol: 4-cylinder DOHC 4-valve with MEMS engine management and multi-point injection. Iron block and alloy cylinder head; five main bearings; belt-driven camshafts. Bore 84.45mm, stroke 89mm, capacity 1994cc. Compression ratio 10:1. Maximum power 134bhp (100kW) at 6000 rpm; maximum torque 137lb. ft (186Nm) at 2500 rpm.

1995-1997 models: torque increased to 140lb.ft (190Nm) at 3600 rpm.

V8 carburettor petrol: Overhead-valve V8 with twin SU carburettors. Alloy block and cylinder heads; five main bearings; chain-driven camshaft. Bore 88.9mm, stroke 71.12mm, capacity 3528cc. Compression ratio 8.13:1. Maximum power 144bhp (108kW) at 5000 rpm; maximum torque 192lb.ft (260Nm) at 2800 rpm. Lower power and torque ratings with optional exhaust catalyst.

V8 injection petrol, 3.5-litre: As above, but with Lucas-Bosch petrol injection. Compression ratio 9.35:1. Maximum power 164bhp (122kW) at 4750 rpm; maximum torque 212lb.ft (288Nm) at 3000 rpm.

Low-compression (8.13:1) engine with exhaust catalyst standard in some markets and optional elsewhere. This engine has maximum power of 153bhp (115kW) and maximum torque of 192lb.ft (260Nm) at the same crankshaft speeds.

V8 petrol, 3.9-litre: As above, but with 93.98mm bore and 3947cc capacity. Compression ratio 9.35:1; exhaust catalyst standard. Maximum power 180bhp (134kW) at 4750 rpm; maximum torque 230lb.ft (312Nm) at 3100 rpm.

On 1995-1998 models, maximum power is 182bhp (135kW) and maximum torque 231lbft (314Nm) at the same crankshaft speeds.

V8 petrol, 4.0-litre (North America only, 1996-1998 models): As above, but with GEMS engine management system, redesigned ancillary drives, separate ignition coils for each cylinder and maximum torque of 233lb.ft. (316Nm).

Transmission

Manual gearbox (1990-1994 models): 5-speed LT77 (1990-1991 models) or LT77S with improved synchromesh (1992-1994 models).

Gear ratios 3.69:1, 2.13:1, 1.40:1, 1.00:1, 0.77:1; reverse 3.43:1. Mpi types have 0.79:1 fifth gear.

Manual gearbox (1995-1998 models): 5-speed R380. Gear ratios (Tdi models) 3.32:1, 2.13:1, 1.40:1, 1.00:1, 0.77:1; reverse 3.43:1. V8 gearboxes have 0.73:1 fifth gear and Mpi types have 0.79:1.

All manual gearboxes drive through a hydraulically-operated 10.5-inch single dry-plate clutch.

Automatic gearbox: 4-speed ZF 4HP22 with lock-up torque converter. Gear ratios 2.48:1, 1.48:1, 1.00:1, 0.73:1; reverse 2.09:1. Not available on Mpi models.

Transfer gearbox: 2-speed LT230T (LT230Q on 1997-1998 NAS models), arranged to deliver permanent 4-wheel drive. Lockable centre differential. Gear ratios 1.22:1 and 3.32:1.

Final drive: 3.54:1 on all models.

Suspension and steering

Live front axle with linear-rate coil springs and hydraulic telescopic dampers, located by radius arms and Panhard rod.

Live rear axle with progressive-rate coil springs and hydraulic telescopic dampers, located by radius arms and A-frame.

Front and rear anti-roll bars optional on 1994 models and standard on 1995-1998 models.

Power-assisted worm-and-roller steering with 3.375 turns lock to lock.

Brakes, wheels and tyres

Disc brakes all round with dual hydraulic circuit on front wheels and servo assistance as standard. Internal expanding drum-type parking brake on transfer box rear output shaft.

Front brakes on 1990-1994 models: 11.77 in (299 mm) diameter solid discs; 1995-1998 models: 11.73 in (298 mm) diameter ventilated discs. Rear discs on all models have 11.42 in (290 mm) diameter.

Steel 16-inch wheels on base models; alloy 16-inch types standard on more expensive models and optional on others.

Tyres: 205 R16 except with Freestyle Choice handling package from mid-1993, which comes with 235/70 R 16 tyres.

Performance

Acceleration, 0-60 mph:

Mpi	15.3 sec
Tdi (manual)	17.2 sec
Tdi (automatic)	18.9 sec
V8 3.5 carb (manual)	12.8 sec
V8i 3.5 injection (manual)	11.7 sec
V8i 3.9 (manual)	10.8 sec
V8i 3.9 (automatic)	11.8 sec

Maximum speed:

Mpi	98 mph
Tdi (manual)	91 mph
Tdi (automatic)	90 mph
V8 3.5 carb (manual)	95 mph
V8i 3.5 injection (manual)	105 mph
V8i 3.9 (manual)	106 mph
V8i 3.9 (automatic)	105 mph

Overall fuel consumption:

Mpi	24 mpg
Tdi (manual)	25 mpg
Tdi (automatic)	24 mpg
V8 3.5 carb (manual)	15 mpg

V8i 3.5 injection (manual) 17 mpg
V8i 3.9 (manual)   20 mpg
V8i 3.9 (automatic)   19 mpg

Dimensions
Length:
1990-94: 4521 mm (178 in)
1995-98: 4538 mm (178.6 in)
Width:
1793 mm (70.6 in) over door mirrors
Height:
1920 mm (75.6 in) without roof bars
1968 mm (77.5 in) with roof bars
Turning circle: 12 metres (39.4 ft)
Kerb weight: Weights vary greatly, depending on specification. A base model Mpi 3-door is the lightest (around 1887kg or 4160lb), while a top-specification Tdi automatic is the heaviest (around 2087kg or 4600lb). An average would be around 1996kg or 4400lb.

Towing capacities
V8, V8i and Tdi: 4000 kg (8800 lb) with fully-braked trailer
3500 kg (7700 lb) with trailer with over-run brakes
750 kg (1650 lb) with unbraked trailer
Mpi: 4000 kg (8800 lb) with fully-braked trailer
2750 kg (6050 lb) with trailer with over-run brakes
750 kg (1650 lb) with unbraked trailer

The five-door was more soberly presented than the three-door, although it had side graphics for some overseas markets. This "compass" design of side graphics arrived on three-doors for the 1992 model-year

Discovery Series II

Chassis

Steel ladder-type frame with box-section members, six cross-members and 14 rubber body mounts

Bodyshell

Steel inner skeleton with steel outer panels; some parts of skeleton and some lower panels zinc-coated. 5-door configuration only.

Engines

Diesel: Td5 5-cylinder with direct injection by electronic unit injectors, turbocharger and intercooler. Iron block and alloy cylinder head; five main bearings; chain-driven camshaft. Bore 85.5mm, stroke 89.0mm, capacity 2495cc. Compression ratio 19.5:1. Maximum power 136bhp (101.5kW) at 4200 rpm; maximum torque 221lb.ft (300Nm) at 1950 rpm with manual gearbox or 232lb.ft (315Nm) with automatic gearbox.

On 2002-2004 models with automatic transmission, torque of the Td5 engine was increased to 250lb.ft (340Nm) at 1950 rpm.

4.0-litre petrol: Overhead-valve V8 with Bosch 5.2.1 fuel and ignition management system. Alloy block and cylinder heads; five main bearings; chain-driven camshaft. Bore 93.98mm, stroke 71.12mm, capacity 3947cc. Compression ratio 9.35:1. Maximum power 182bhp (136kW) at 4750 rpm; maximum torque 250lb.ft (340 Nm) at 2600 rpm.

4.6-litre petrol: As above, but with 82mm stroke and 4554cc capacity. Compression ratio 9.37:1. Maximum power 217bhp (162kW) at 4750 rpm; maximum torque 300lb.ft (407Nm) at 2600 rpm.

Transmission

Manual gearbox: 5-speed R380. Gear ratios (Td5 models) 3.69:1, 2.13:1, 1.40:1, 1.00:1, 0.77:1; reverse 3.54:1. V8 gearboxes had 3.32:1 first gear and 0.73:1 fifth gear.

All manual gearboxes drove through a hydraulically-operated 10.5-inch single dry-plate clutch.

Automatic: 4-speed ZF 4HP22 with lock-up torque converter. Gear ratios 2.48:1, 1.48:1, 1.00:1, 0.73:1, reverse 2.09:1.

On 2003-2004 North American models with the 4.6-litre V8 engine, a stronger 4HP24 gearbox was used. The gear ratios were the same as on other automatics.

Transfer gearbox: 2-speed LT230SE, arranged to deliver permanent 4-wheel drive. Centre differential manually lockable on some 2003-2004 models. Gear ratios 1.21:1 and 3.27:1.

Final drive: 3.54:1 on all models.

Suspension and steering

Live front axle with coil springs and twin-tube hydraulic telescopic dampers, located by longitudinal radius arms; 30mm anti roll bar or ACE anti-roll system, depending on model.

Live rear axle with coil springs or air springs (depending on model) and twin-tube hydraulic telescopic dampers; located by longitudinal radius arms and Watts linkage; 19mm anti-roll bar with coil springs, 29mm anti-roll-bar with air springs.

Power-assisted worm-and-roller steering, with 3.5 turns from lock to lock.

Brakes, wheels and tyres

Disc brakes on all four wheels with dual hydraulic circuit on front wheels and servo assistance as standard. Internal expanding drum-type parking brake on transfer box rear output shaft.

1999-2002 models have 11.81in (300mm) diameter discs, ventilated at front; 2003-2004 models have 11.7in (297mm) at the front and 11.97in (304mm) at the rear. ABS is standard, together with EBD and HDC.

Steel 16-inch wheels on entry-level models and Commercials; alloy 16-inch and 18-inch types standard on more expensive models.

Standard tyre sizes are 235 R16 on cheaper models and 255/65 R16 on more expensive types. Optional tyre sizes are 215 R16 and 255/55 R18.

Performance

Acceleration, 0-60 mph:

Td5 (manual)	14.2 secs
Td5 (automatic)	15.8 secs
4.0 V8 (manual)	10.9 secs
4.0 V8 (automatic)	11.9 secs
4.6 V8 (automatic)	9.5 secs

Maximum speed:

Td5 (manual and auto)	98 mph
4.0 V8 (manual and auto)	106 mph
4.6 V8 (automatic)	Not quoted

Overall fuel consumption:

Td5 (manual)	30.1 mpg
Td5 (automatic)	27.4 mpg
4.0 V8 (manual)	17.0 mpg
4.0 V8 (automatic)	16.9 mpg
4.6 V8 (automatic)	16.0mpg (US galls)

Dimensions

Length: 4705 mm (185.2 in)
Width: 1890 mm (74.4 in) over door mirrors
Height: 1940 mm (76.4 in) with roof bars
Turning circle: 11.9 metres (39 ft)
Kerb weight: Weights vary greatly, depending on specification. A 4.0 V8 model with rear coil springs and basic trim is the lightest, with an EC Unladen Weight of 2020kg (4453lb). The heaviest, at 2205kg (4861lb) is a Td5 with ACE, SLS and the top level of trim. An average would be around 2112kg (4657lb).

Towing capacities

All models: 3500 kg (7700 lb) with trailer with over-run brakes

750 kg (1650 lb) with unbraked trailer

Discovery background

There's no doubt that the Discovery has become the core model of the Land Rover range. More practical than the utility models that had their origins as commercial vehicles, more spacious and rugged than the Freelander, and more affordable than the Range Rover, it is a proper dual-purpose vehicle. A great towcar and family holdall, it is equally at home taking Dad to work or the kids to school, while at weekends it can cut the mustard in demanding off-road entertainment.

However, its story goes back only to the 1980s, by which time the Land Rover marque was preparing to celebrate its 40th anniversary and the Range Rover was already a decade and a half old. The Discovery was Land Rover's calculated response to a market opportunity that had been very successfully exploited by Japanese manufacturers such as Mitsubishi and Isuzu. This market opportunity was for a Range Rover-like 4x4 estate car at a cheaper price, offering family versatility and practicality.

The Mitsubishi Shogun (Pajero in some markets) and Isuzu Trooper (Rodeo in some markets) had arrived at the start of the 1980s. Together with a small number of others, they had quickly dominated the family 4x4 market. Land Rover, meanwhile, was going through a difficult period after its traditional market for utility models in Africa had collapsed – again under a Japanese onslaught. Its Managing Director, Tony Gilroy, recognised that the best option for long-term survival was to focus on passenger vehicles for developed countries rather than on utility

models for the Third World. As a result, the Range Rover was prepared for North America and was launched there in 1987, and the company also began to look at ways of tackling the family 4x4 market.

One problem was that Land Rover had left it very late. Their business analysts assessed that they needed to be in the market with a class-leading product by mid-1989 in order to stand a chance of weathering the hard times.

The typical development time for an all-new model would have taken the company past that deadline, and so it became imperative to draw on existing production hardware. In addition, the company decided to pioneer new working practices that would dramatically reduce the design and development time for a new model.

The solution was to use the existing Range Rover chassis and drivetrain, supplemented by a new diesel engine that was already under development. The whole would be clothed in a distinctive new body that would be carefully designed to suit the family market.

Following Japanese practice, there would be two versions of the new vehicle, a 2-door to appeal to younger people and a 4-door to appeal to the family market. Unlike the Japanese, however, and in order to save money, Land Rover decided to put both bodies onto exactly the same chassis.

Project Jay was announced as the Land Rover Discovery in autumn 1989 and very quickly took over the number one best-seller position in the European 4x4 market. This rapid success was undoubtedly helped by Land Rover's launch strategy of introduc-ing the 2-door model first (called a 3-door

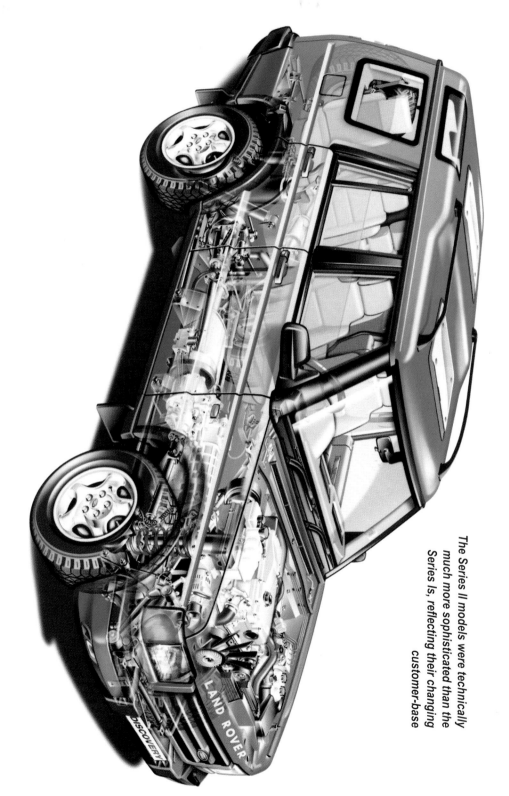

The Series II models were technically much more sophisticated than the Series Is, reflecting their changing customer-base

The original Series II models had a front end with rectangular lights and a body-coloured lower frame for the grille

because of its large tail door) in order to give the vehicle a young, "lifestyle-oriented" image. A year later came the rather more soberly appointed 4-door ("5-door") model with its greater family practicality. Both models came as 5-seaters, but a very popular option was a pair of inward-facing occasional seats in the load bed. Thus configured as a 7-seater, the Discovery was bound to appeal to larger families and to the developing MPV market.

The Discovery retained its position as the best-selling 4x4 in Europe until the end of Series I production, when it ceded that title to Land Rover's own newcomer, the Freelander.

The overwhelming favourite was always the Tdi diesel engine, which offered good fuel economy to make the vehicle more affordable as an everyday proposition. The V8 petrol alternatives, meanwhile, were always very thirsty (if much more refined

than the diesels) and were only really popular in countries with low fuel costs, such as North America.

In fact, North America didn't get the Discovery until 1994. The model was redeveloped to meet the requirements of that market at the same time as it was being given its mid-life facelift. However, the Discovery was marketed as a "premium" model in North America and this, together with Land Rover's relatively small number of dealerships, ensured that the Discovery would only ever be a bit-part player on the far side of the Atlantic.

Land Rover introduced a new top model with additional luxury equipment when the Series I models had their mid-life facelift, moving the Discovery range upwards into territory vacated by the Range Rover which, in tun, had become more expensive. Sales of the cheaper models declined, mainly under the impact of the new Freelander.

As a result, the Series II Discovery that was launched in 1998 as a 1999 model was really a more up-market vehicle than the older model had been. The customers it was aimed at had no interest in a 3-door model, and so the Series II was only ever built in 5-door form.

It was also more complex, featuring a host of sophisticated electronic systems for its engine management, traction control systems, and even suspension. Engines "talked" to automatic gearboxes to give smoother gear changes, and there was an impressive new heating, ventilating and air conditioning system with automatic temperature control.

Yet the Series II Discovery was still very clearly a Discovery in its overall appearance and in its practical appeal as an everyday family vehicle.

It continued to use "old" technology in its separate-chassis construction and beam axles; and it continued to sell strongly. Once again, the diesel engine – now the Td5 type – was the strong seller outside North America, which only took V8s.

Like the Series I models, the Series IIs were facelifted, although this time way beyond the mid-point of their production run. After four years in production, and with two years to go, they were given new front and rear details and a cosmetic makeover.

North America had the additional benefit of a larger-capacity V8 engine for these last two seasons of production, although that engine was not made available in other markets. These final models – for 2003 and 2004 – didn't carry the oval "Series II" badge on their tailgates. Although in the strict sense they were Series II models, Land Rover always preferred to call them 2003 models or 2004 models.

When production finally came to an end, on May 27, 2004, the successor to the Series II models had already been announced. Known as the Discovery 3, it took the model even further up-market and embodied a wide range of sophisticated new technology.

The 2004 models had raised lettering on the bonnet in place of the flat decals used earlier

Discovery Series I
Model changes

This section summarises the major specification changes that Land Rover made to the Discovery Series I during its nine year production life. Its primary aim is to help you identify the different versions of the model.

Chassis frame

The chassis frame of the Series I Discovery is essentially that of the original Range Rover, and it remained unchanged except in minor details throughout Series I production.

Bodyshell

The Discovery's bodyshell shares its basic construction principles with that of the first-generation Range Rover. There's a load-bearing steel inner skeleton, and the outer aluminium panels are unstressed. Unlike the Range Rover, the Discovery has a steel roof that is welded to the skeleton frame for extra rigidity.

Just like the Range Rover, the Discovery can suffer from electrolytic action where steel and alloy meet. While rust protection is generally pretty good (all that experience with early Range Rovers had taught Land Rover a lot), the steel inner skeleton can start to rust and the alloy panels can corrode into white powder.

The Series I Discoverys were available in 3-door and 5-door configurations. There's no difference in the basic structures, but the bodysides are different pressings. The big tail door was designed both to help distinguish the model from the Range Rover whose underpinnings it used, and to give more practical access to the load bay for both occasional-seat passengers and the week's shopping. Unfortunately, it was hinged on the wrong side to suit buyers in LHD markets, acting as a barrier between the load bay and the kerb when it was opened. Not that this seems to have hindered sales very much!

For the UK market, 3-door models generally had bodyside graphics in the shape of large decals. For 1990 and 1991, these were essentially horizontal stripes, and from 1992 to 1994 , there was a "compass" design. As time went on, however, more and more customers asked for the decals to be left off. Models for other markets often had different bodyside graphics.

5-door models did not have these graphics in the UK, although 5-doors for some overseas markets had special bodyside decals. In the UK, 5-doors were generally more soberly presented, with nothing more than a "Discovery" decal on each front wing and the usual tail door badges.

The 1995 model-year facelift brought new front and rear details for the Discovery's bodyshell. The original Sherpa van headlamps were replaced by more carefully styled rectangular units, and the front apron was restyled to look more substantial. There were new wraparounds for the front and rear bumper ends, and the rear bumper now incorporated the turn indicator and fog guard lights. The light clusters on the rear body pillars were redesigned without these two items, but many customers objected and so Land Rover offered a kit to fit the earlier rear light clusters. Discoverys so converted ended up with two sets of turn indicators at the rear, plus two sets of fog guard lights. It appears that these "dual" rear lights became standard on NAS Discoverys, but it is not clear when.

The original dashboard was functional but rather spartan. For 1990, all interiors were in Sonar Blue

Equipment and accessories

Early Discoverys were pretty sparsely equipped, mainly to keep entry-level prices down. However, there was a huge variety of accessories on offer, and Land Rover made a particular point of this. The idea was that every customer could specifiy the vehicle to suit his or her lifestyle very precisely – and of course the extras could bump up showroom prices and profits by a considerable margin.

Most Series I Discoverys had roof rails, although these were deleted from cheaper models. Their purpose is largely cosmetic, and few people use the optional cross-bars which turn them into a roof rack. Although large numbers of Discoverys do have sunroofs, these were by no means standard. The twin-sunroof feature (one for the front passengers, one for those in the back) was one of the selling points on the early models. You could buy air conditioning and electric windows from the beginning, although the more sophisticated heating and air

conditioning system with separate controls for driver and passenger didn't arrive until the mid-life facelift in March 1994. The steering column wasn't height-adjustable until then, either, and nor were airbags available. Many Discoverys continued to be sold without airbags at all, or with only a driver's airbag (when the passenger's side airbag space was used for an open shelf with a grab handle).

From December 1996, a bodykit known as Bodystyle Choice was added to the accessories list. This consisted of a restyled front apron and side sills, but sold very poorly in the UK and is rare today.

Steel wheels were standard on the first Discoverys, and remained available on entry-level models until the end of Series I production. However, alloy wheels made their appearance as accessories during 1990, and gradually became an important part of the Series I Discovery's specification. There is a list of the different types near the end of this section.

Twin sunroofs were another optional extra, initially always manually operated but later with a power operation option

Interior

The Discovery's interior was designed fromn the outset to be practical, and always used hard-wearing fabrics for the seats and tough plastics for the dash and door trims. The distinctive dimpled "golf ball" textures on grab handles and steering wheel were all part of the model's character, and there was an abundance of places to stow the sort of clutter that a family usually carries around in its car.

For example, there were map stowage pockets above the sun visors, and retaining nets in the headlining just above the rear seat. In five-seaters, there were deep stowage bins in the sides of the load bay, and all models had deep, rigid door pockets. The tops of the dash and the centre console were flat, too, so that oddments could be put on them. It was unfortunate that a useful stowage pocket on the passenger's side of the dash disappeared if the optional air conditioning was fitted.

A key element in the Discovery's appeal was that it was available optionally with seven seats – five facing forwards conventionally and two facing inwards at the rear. The rearmost pair were designed primarily for children, as they offered insufficient legroom for adults. They could be folded up out of the way to clear the load area. Five seat models had large oddments bins in place of these seats; seven seaters always came with a spring-loaded retractable rear step to enable the occupants of the two rearmost seats to climb in through the tail door.

Over the first five years of production – throughout the 200-series era – there were very few changes to the interior. However, you'll see that 1991 and later model dashboards have a side-window demister outlet at each end of the dashboard, while the first year's models don't. From 1997, it was possible to order a rear air condition- ing option. This is rare, perhaps not least because it consists of a large and rather ugly

The dashboard was heavily revised for the 300-series models. This example shows the twin-airbag installation

This spring loaded folding step was fitted to aid access to the rearmost seats on seven-seater models

If no driver's side airbag was fitted, this style of steering wheel was used on 300-series models

box-like structure added to the back of the centre console.

On 200-series Discoverys, the seats were invariably upholstered in fabric. There was Sonar Blue from the beginning, supplemented by the rather more sober Bahama Beige when five-door models arrived for 1991. The blue disappeared on 300-series models, being replaced by grey. You could order leather upholstery on the 300-series Discoverys, too, in the usual grey or beige. Right at the end of Series I production, the Premium trim option brought very attractive Lightstone (light beige) leather. The sporty trim used on some derivatives from the 1996 model-year (such as the XS in the UK) combined leather side bolsters with cloth seat wearing surfaces featuring bold Land Rover logos. All rear seats were arranged with a 60-40 split, to maximise the vehicle's carrying capacity.

While 200-series interiors are quite brash, especially in Sonar Blue, those of the 300-series models are much more sophisticated and reflect the tastes of the family market the model was aimed at.

Engines

Right from the start, the key engines in most markets were the diesels. North America took only petrol V8s, but these accounted for only a small proportion of sales in other countries because of their high fuel consumption. It's no surprise that in the UK, large numbers of early V8 Discoverys have either been converted to run on LPG (with attendant fuel cost advantages) or retrofitted with diesel engines.

The V8 petrol engines do bring a refinement to the Discovery which the diesels simply cannot match. For the first year of Discovery

The V8 engines were never very popular in the UK on account of their high fuel consumption, but they did bring a degree of refinement that the Tdi lacked. This is a 3.9-litre type

production, V8 engines had a 3.5-litre swept volume and twin SU carburettors, and the models they powered wore V8 badges. With the arrival of 5-door Discoverys for the 1991 model-year, however, the engine switched to fuel injection, which brought a gain in power and allowed the engine to be more easily re-tuned to meet exhaust emissions regulations in some export territories. These later models were badged as V8i types. Some had catalytic converters, and in the UK these were rare enough to have an identifying badge on the tail door.

The next stage was a switch to the 3.9-litre swept volume which the Range Rover had already pioneered. Discoverys got the bigger engine for the 1994 model year, and stayed with it right through to the end of Series I production. There were various changes in power and torque output over the years, dictated by minor re-tuning to meet changing emissions regulations, but none of any real significance. These models retained the V8i badging.

North America, though, was an exception. While its 1994-1995 models had the 3.9-litre V8, the 1996-1998 models had the redeveloped engine that was known as the 4.0-litre. It actually had the same swept volume, power and torque as the 3.9-litre type, but had been redeveloped in some areas to suit the second-generation Range Rover introduced in 1994. To simplify the job of meeting US homologation regulations and to streamline their own spares stocks, Land Rover fitted it to Discoverys for the US and Canada as well.

The Discovery was the first Land Rover to have the brand-new 200 Tdi diesel engine. In fact, it wasn't quite as new as publicity suggested, because its block was derived from that of the old 2.5-litre Land Rover diesel – a design which could trace its origins back to the mid-1950s! However, the engine used the very latest technology to achieve excellent fuel economy and performance. Direct injection, traditionally the preserve of buses and trucks because of its high noise

The 300 Tdi was a more refined engine than the original 200 Tdi, but there was no mistaking that it was a diesel; yellow oil filler cap and large black soundproofing cover are identifying features

levels, provided the economy. Performance came from the use of a turbocharger. And both goals were served by the use of an intercooler to cool the air injected into the combustion chambers for maximum efficiency. The name of 200 Tdi came from those key design features – Turbocharged, Direct injection and Intercooled – while the 200 was an approximation of its very high maximum torque of 195 lb.ft. (264Nm).

This engine was redeveloped as the 300 Tdi for the 1995 model-year, with no fewer than 208 new components. Noise levels dropped to a very noticeable degree, raising refinement and keeping the engine competitive with newer designs from other manufacturers. There was no extra power or torque (the 300 in its name was pure marketing-speak), although for the 1996 model year the engines in automatic Discoverys were uprated to improve top-end performance. These engines also had electronic management units to keep exhaust emissions within the legally required limits.

There was a third engine, too, although it was available only for the 1994-1997 model years. This was the Mpi, a high-revving 2.0-litre petrol engine originally designed for transverse use in Rover cars. This gave reasonable fuel economy plus the refinement of a petrol engine, and had the benefit of being small enough to get under various tax barriers in the overseas markets for which it was mainly intended.

Transmission

Every Series I Discovery has a two-speed transfer gearbox, with a high ratio for on-road driving and a low ratio which gears down the output of the primary gearbox to give a range of crawler gears for off-road use. This transfer gearbox – the LT230 – also splits the drive 50-50 between front and rear axles, delivering Land Rover's trademark permanent four-wheel drive. Front and rear axles on all Series I models have the same 3.54:1 final drive gearing.

All Discoverys had LT77 5-speed manual gearboxes for the model's first three years, the 1992 model year bringing the LT77S improved synchromesh to overcome difficult engagement of first and second gears when cold. For 1995, a completely new 5-speed manual gearbox was introduced. Called the R380, this had a different gate pattern, with reverse behind fifth instead of out beside first. It also offered much smoother, slicker changes. Many early R380s gave trouble, although they were dealt with under warranty and shouldn't be a cause for concern now.

The alternative gearbox was a 4-speed automatic made by ZF in Germany, and known as the 4 HP 22. It had been used in Range Rovers for many years before becoming available on 1993-model V8i Discoverys. The automatic was also made available with the diesel engine for 1994, but it was never offered with the Mpi.

Early Discoverys had a conventional UJ in the rear propshaft, but 300-series models had a rubber doughnut coupling, which was intended to reduce noise transmission. Land Rover always described this as a "decoupled" rear propshaft."

Suspension and steering

Series I Discoverys had the proven Range Rover power-assisted worm and roller steering. They used the Range Rover's suspension, too, but with stiffer coil springs at the rear in place of a self-levelling strut.

All this gave the Discovery a fairly comfortable ride but a prodigious amount of body roll, so an anti-roll bar package was made available on 1994 models and standardised on 300-series models. Again pioneered on the Range Rover, it was re-tuned to suit the Discovery's characteristics. During the 1994 model year, it was marketed as part of the Freestyle Choice option package, with stylish alloy wheels and lower-profile tyres.

The first automatics appeared for the 1993 model year

Brakes, wheels and tyres

Early Discoverys had solid-rotor disc brakes all round with power assistance as standard and a dual hydraulic circuit for the front wheels. On the 300-series models, the front brakes were upgraded with ventilated rotors. In typical Land Rover fashion, the handbrake didn't operate on the rear wheels but on the rear propshaft, where it was less vulnerable to problems caused by mud and debris picked up during off-road use.

Early 16-inch diameter steel wheel

5-spoke alloy as fitted to first 5-door cars

Freestyle alloy with 'star' pattern spokes

Freestyle with grey enamel finish

Factory-fit wheels on Series I Discoverys always had a 16-inch diameter (nevertheless one German limited edition had a 15-inch type fitted by the importers).

Entry-level models had styled steel wheels, but various alloy types were soon introduced, both for more expensive variants and as options. Most later models were supplied with alloys of one sort or another, and a full list of the different types is given below.

Styled steel
Silver finish, perforated disc wheel
5-spoke option
First alloy wheel option; five flat spokes
5-door alloy
5-spoke alloy wheel with "chunky" spokes
Freestyle alloy
Five spokes in star pattern
Enamelled Freestyle alloy
As above, but spokes with dark grey enamel finish
Castor alloy
5-spoke design with pronounced circular centre section, seen on 300-series models
Deep Dish alloy
5-spoke design with deep recessed centre
Boost alloy
Five flat spokes, each with raised edges
Tornado alloy
Similar to Freestyle, but with flatter spokes

Tyres were always 205R16 radials, except with the Freestyle Choice handling package, which brought 235/70R16s. Factory-fit tyres were always dual-purpose with a bias towards road use. Heavy-duty off-road driving really requires tyres with a more aggressive tread pattern (which will be noisier on the road).

5-spoke Castor alloy wheel

Tornado style alloy wheel

5-spoke Deep Dish alloy wheel

5-spoke Boost alloy wheel

Model designations

Land Rover used different model designations in different markets, and it isn't possible to include every different nomenclature here. So the data below relates only to the Discovery's two main markets of the UK and North America.

200-series

For the 1990-1992 model-years, Discoverys were simply known as 3-door or 5-door types in the UK. Then from May 1992, a stripped-out 5-door Tdi was introduced to meet new company car tax regulations. 5-door models with the earlier and more comprehensive specification were now re-named Discovery S types, but never carried identifying badges. 3-door, 5-door and 5-door S remained available for the 1993-1994 model years.

300-series

For the 1995 model-year, the range consisted of five models. The entry-level 3-door and 5-door models were generally known simply as "estates". Above them were the mid-range 3-door and 5-door S models, as before devoid of identifying badges. At the top of the range was the ES, available as a 5-door only and carrying ES decals on the front wings and tailgate.

For the 1996 and 1997 model years, the five model range was supplemented by a sixth model. This was the XS 5-door, a supposedly sporty variant which fitted between the S and ES types in the Discovery hierarchy.

The 1998 model year brought a further expanded range, although by this stage there were very few 3-door models. There were now eight different types. Both 3-doors and 5-doors could be had in Estate, GS and XS trim. Above these were ES 5-doors and ES Premium 5-door models (the latter with Lightstone leather upholstery). GS, XS, ES and ES Premium models all carried appropriate badges on front wings and tail door.

North America

The 1994-1995 North American specification Discoverys were all 5-doors, the only model choice being between 5-seat and 7-seat configurations.

For 1996-1997, the models were renamed and specifications were upgraded. Entry-level types, usually with manual transmission, wore SD badges. The mid-range model was the SE, with leather upholstery and automatic transmission as standard. Top of the range was the SE7, which came with seven seats and rear air conditioning. Like the SD, the SE and SE7 wore appropriate badges on front wings and tailgate.

For 1998, Canada had an entry-level SD model (now with automatic transmission) but the US did not. Both territories took the LE (with five or seven seats) and the better-equipped LSE with chrome bumpers and body-coloured end caps, door mirrors, grille and apron. All models had wing and tailgate badges.

There were also a few "carry-over" models badged as SD and sold alongside the Series II Discovery in the early months of the 1999 model-year.

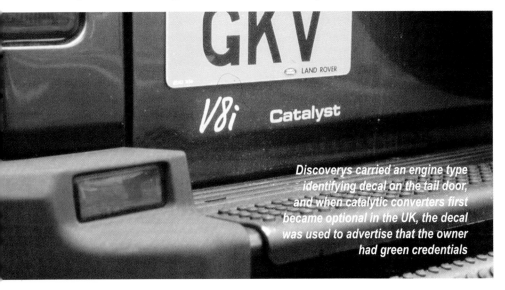

Discoverys carried an engine type identifying decal on the tail door, and when catalytic converters first became optional in the UK, the decal was used to advertise that the owner had green credentials

Discovery Series II
Model changes

In this section, you'll find the major specification changes that Land Rover made to the Series II Discovery. There were nowhere near as many as during the longer production life of the Series I models. The Series II was on sale for just six years, and by this stage Land Rover had a much clearer understanding of the Discovery's potential customers and targeted them more precisely and effectively.

Chassis frame

The Series II's steel ladder-frame chassis had been redesigned specially for the vehicle. Although the wheelbase remained the same as before, at 100 inches, the new chassis frame was actually longer, having been extended behind the rear axle to allow for a longer body.

Bodyshell

The Discovery Series II retained the stepped roof, upright rear and side-opening tail door which had characterised the first-generation models. There were very noticeable differences, though: the rearmost side windows and the Alpine roof lights, for example, were flush-glazed and their glass was bonded to the bodyshell. This increased rigidity and reduced wind noise and leaks. The new model featured some 200 new pressings and 100 items which had been carried over or modified from the Series I Discovery.

The Series II's bodyshell had far more steel than its predecessor, mainly because steel allowed greater accuracy of panel dimensions than aluminium alloy, which in turn gave more consistent panel gaps. To inhibit rusting, vulnerable areas of the body's inner skeleton and most of the lower exterior panels were made of zinc-coated steel.

All Series IIs had five-door bodies, reflecting customer demand and the new model's positioning in a higher price bracket than the old. Wider tyres were standard on more expensive models, and their extra width was covered by black plastic wheelarch "eyebrows". These underlined the family link between the Discovery and the Defender utilities.

The Series II models' mid-life facelift actually came rather late in their life, arriving for the 2003 models and lasting for two years out of a total six for the model. It brought new "pocket" style headlamp units similar to those recently introduced on the third-generation Range Rover, plus a redesigned front apron which was far less vulnerable and gave a better approach angle in off-road use. Driving lamps were relocated in the face of the bumper. At the back, the main light clusters in the body pillars were redesigned with smooth lenses and incorporated the turn indicators, while the reversing lamps moved down to the rear bumper. For 2004, the Land Rover name on the bonnet changed from a flat decal to the raised lettering introduced with the third generation Range Rover in 2002.

New child seat locking systems arrived on these later Discoverys, North American models getting the LATCH system for 2003 and UK models getting the ISOFIX system for 2004. A new option for 2003 was thicker "Aero" roof bars, and these were standardised on some 2004 models. Also introduced on 2003 North American models was automatic locking of all the doors when the vehicle reached 4 mph (7 km/h). This was carried over to UK models for the 2004 model year.

Note that the 2003 and 2004 models didn't carry the "Series II" oval badge which had been used since the start of Series II Discovery production. Although they were Series II models in the strict sense of the term, Land Rover always preferred to call them "2003 models" or "2004 models". In North America, where the 4.6-litre V8 engine became standard, they were usually called "4.6" models.

Equipment and accessories

Land Rover moved the Discovery Series II into a higher price bracket than the one occupied by the Series I models, in order not to damage sales of the new Freelander which had reached the showrooms at the start of 1998. So entry-level Discoverys with low equipment levels were not very common in the model's major markets. Most Series II models have relatively high levels of equipment as compared to their Series I counterparts.

A wide range of accessories was available, and Land Rover used some of these to help create attractive limited-edition models. For more details, see Special Models (page 41).

Interior

Like the original Discovery, the Series II could have either five or seven seats. However, the two "occasional" seats in the rear loadspace now faced forwards instead of inwards and had full 3-point safety harnesses. The front seats were wider and there were adjustable head restraints on the front and centre rows of seats; for the rear passengers, headrests pulled down from the roof when the seats were in use. The centre passenger in the second row of seats had a headrest, which sank down out of the way when the armrest was down. Those second row seats had a 60-40 split fold, as before.

On the 1999-2000 models, there were three upholstery styles for most territories, featuring cloth, leather or part-leather (on

The Series II dashboard was generally similar to the type designed for 300-series Discoverys, but had been further refined

This is the full seven seater version of the Series II, with the Lightstone leather upholstery and extra wood trim of the Premium interior specification

sporty models such as the XS). Standard colours were grey and beige, but Lightstone leather was also available as an option. The full-leather trim on top models came with contrast piping and Alcantara accent panels on the door casings. North America switched to Duragrain PVC upholstery in place of cloth during the 2000 model-year, but this option was not available in other markets.

When the ATC system was not fitted, there were rotary dials for the heating and ventilation controls

On the 2001 and 2002 models, a fourth combination of cloth upholstery with leather bolsters was available on the Adventurer model in the UK. This combination was abandoned for the 2003 and 2004 model years, when a new range of three interior colours was made available.

Traces of the earlier "golf-ball" textures were still evident on grab handles and the like, and the Series II once again had a variety of stowage places for oddments and clutter.

The Series II dashboard was very similar to the 300-era Series I type, and on top models came with a heating and air conditioning system which featured automatic temperature control. You simply set the temperature you wanted, and the system would automatically maintain that temperature in the cabin; as before, there were separate controls for the driver's and passenger's sides of the vehicle.

The Td5 engine is usually concealed under a large black plastic cover. This is what it looks like without in the bare chassis

Rear air conditioning became available some time after production had started, and was now integrated properly into the vehicle with outlet vents in the headlining above the rear seating area.

Engines

In the beginning, the Series II Discovery was available with only two engine options. These were a redeveloped 4.0-litre petrol V8 and a brand-new five-cylinder diesel known as the Td5. For the 2003 and 2004 model years, North America had a 4.6-litre V8 instead of the 4.0-litre derivative.

Most important was the Td5 diesel, its five cylinders delivering greater smoothness and refinement than the superseded 4-cylinder 300Tdi. It boasted the expected low speed torque but also gave a much extended spread of torque and a relatively high rev limit of 4850 rpm. Using a turbocharger, intercooler and direct injection once again,

the Td5 also featured Electronic Unit Injectors – one per cylinder – to provide the optimum fuel delivery at extremely high pressures. All this of course was controlled by an electronic engine management unit, which made the engine less of a DIY dream than the earlier Discovery diesels.

The redeveloped V8 engine was known as the Thor type and also went into Range

The petrol engine option was always the Thor version of the long-serving V8, in 4.0-litre form for most markets until the 2003 model year

For 2003 and 2004 the 4.0 V8 was replaced by the more powerful 4.6-litre derivative on North American models

Rovers for 1999. It featured a new and more compact inlet manifold distinguished by its gracefully curved induction tracts, cross-bolted main bearing caps and a new structural cast alloy sump. The ancillary drive arrangements reflected those seen on the 4.0-litre engine used in North American Series I Discoverys, as did the use of a separate ignition coil for each cylinder. A Bosch engine management system replaced the earlier GEMS type, and the overall results were better refinement and a broader torque curve.

The Thor version of the Range Rover's 4.6-litre V8 was the engine that went into North American Discoverys for 2003-4. It provided more power and torque, and slightly better performance – although in everyday driving the difference was not readily noticeable.

All 2003 and 2004 V8 models had re-routed exhaust systems, which reduced noise levels.

Transmission

As before, Land Rover offered Discovery buyers the choice between a 5-speed manual gearbox and a 4-speed automatic. The 5-speed manual was always the R380 type, and the automatic was always the well-proven ZF unit, now with dual-mode control. The 4.6-litre North American Dicoverys used the stronger version of the ZF gearbox seen earlier on 4.6-litre Range Rovers.

Both primary gearboxes drove through a 2-speed transfer gearbox – this time a version of the earlier LT230 type known as the LT230SE. This of course gave permanent 4-wheel drive as well as a choice of high or low ratios.

However, in the first Series II Discoverys, the centre differential could not be locked manually to give better traction in difficult going. The vehicle instead relied on 4-wheel ETC (Electronic Traction Control) which operated through the standard ABS system.

In most circumstances, it performed superbly, but as a reactive rather than pro-active system it could allow the vehicle to bog down in certain types of terrain. So in response to demand, Land Rover introduced a manually lockable centre differential as an option on the 2003 models. This feature was also standardised on the 2003 and 2004 Discoverys for North America.

(Ironically, all the hardware for the manually lockable centre differential was present in the transfer box on most earlier Discoverys; it simply wasn't connected to a lever. Some 2002 models had a transfer box without this hardware, but the earlier design was reinstated when a manual lock became optional.)

All Series II Discoverys had two electronic traction control systems which added to the capabilities of their transmissions. These were 4-wheel ETC (mentioned above) and HDC (Hill Descent Control). HDC had been pioneered on the Freelander and operated through the ABS system by pulsing the brakes to prevent the vehicle exceeding a set speed when descending a slope off-road. It was operated by a yellow switch on the Discovery's dashboard.

Suspension and steering

The beam axles of Series IIs had wider tracks to give greater stability. There were twin-tube dampers all round, and the location of both axles was by longitudinal radius arms, plus a Watts linkage on the rear. Changed suspension geometry through revised location points gave slightly better handling on the 2003-2004 models.

Base-model Series IIs had all-round coil springs with anti-roll bars, but these could be supplemented by ACE at the front and

The ACE system consisted of hydraulic rams which 'stiffened' the front anti-roll bar

replaced by SLS at the rear, and Land Rover played tunes with the specification options this provided. ACE (Active Cornering Enhancement) was a sophisticated computer-controlled anti-roll system for the front axle. SLS (Self Levelling Suspension) was derived from the height-adjustable air springs used on the Range Rover and brought height-adjustable air springs with automatic load-levelling for the rear axle.

The steering was again a worm-and-roller type with power assistance as standard.

Pursuit (in North America this is called Meteor) wheel

Lightning alloy wheel

Style 1 5-spoke alloy wheel

Brakes, wheels and tyres

Series II brake discs were larger than Series I types, and the front discs were always ventilated. The 2003 and 2004 models had re-sized discs with different front calipers and different pad material, leading to vastly improved braking feel and better response. ABS was always standard with, as noted above, EBD and HDC.

All Series II models had 16-inch wheels in the beginning, with perforated steel discs on entry-level models (and, later, on Commercials) and alloys elsewhere. There were 18-inch alloys available at extra cost, and these larger-diameter wheels were standardised on more expensive models from the start of the 2002 model-year; new alloy wheel designs then appeared for 2003 and continued into 2004. The list of wheel types is given below.

16-inch types

Styled steel: Silver painted disc wheel with perforated outer edge. All model years.

Firestar alloy (US: Mirage): 5-spoke design with "waisted" spokes; 8-inch rim; 1999 and 2000 MYs.

Polar alloy: Five spokes with deep grooves; 7-inch rim; 2001 and 2002 MYs.

Pursuit alloy (In North America: Meteor): Five spokes, each with a raised rib; 7-inch rim; 1999 and 2000 MYs.

Tempest alloy: Five flat spokes, curving in to meet rim; 7-inch rim; 1999-2002 MYs

Stratos alloy: Five "fat" spokes; 8-inch rim; 1999 and 2000 MYs (also 2001 MY for NA).

Typhoon alloy: Duotone finish with five grey enamel spokes and unpainted rim; 8-inch rim 2001 and 2002 MYs.

Lightning alloy: Five narrow spokes with a

line indentation in each; 8-inch rim; 2001 MY, and earlier special editions

Style 1 alloy: Five spokes, each with a wide groove; 7-inch rim; 2003 and 2004 MYs.

Style 2 alloy: Five spokes, each with a cut-out centre; 7-inch rim; 2003 and 2004 MYs.

Style 3 alloy: Six flat spokes; 8-inch rim; 2003 and 2004 MYs.

Style 4 alloy: Five flat spokes with scalloped sections near wheel centre and dark grey finish; 8-inch rim; 2003 and 2004 MYs.

18-inch types

Hurricane: Five split spokes; 8-inch rim; 2002 MY

Mondial: Large star pattern with five spokes; 8-inch rim; 2000 and 2001 MYs.

Triple Sport alloy: Three spokes, each split into two; 8-inch rim; 1999-2002 MYs; accessory fit only.

Pro-Sport alloy (In North America: Proline): Five spokes, each with a styled groove; 8-inch rim; 1999-2002 MYs.

Style 5 alloy: Five divided spokes; 8-inch rim; 2003 and 2004 MYs.

Style 6 alloy: Six flat spokes, similar to Style 3; 8-inch rim; 2003 and 2004 MYs.

Style 7 alloy: Three flat spokes, each divided into two; 8-inch rim; 2003 and 2004 MYs.

Tyres were once again road-biased dual-purpose types with limited off-road capabilities. Steel wheels came with 205R16 tyres; other entry-level models had 235R16s on 7-inch alloy rims.

There were wider tyres on 8-inch rims for more expensive models, and these made the wheelarch eyebrows necessary: the tyres were 255/65s with 16-inch wheels or 255/55s with 18-inch types.

Style 3 6-spoke alloy wheel

Pro-Sport (in North America this is called Proline) alloy wheel

Style 5 alloy wheel

Model designations

As with the Series I models, the data given here relates to the Series II Discovery's two main markets of the UK and North America. The specifications for other countries were either the same as, or variations of, these.

UK market

For MY 1999 and 2000, the basic UK range consisted of entry-level S, mid-range GS, sporty XS and luxury ES models. For 2001 and 2002, the model-range was enlarged to six types with the addition of a cheaper entry-level E model and of the Adventurer at a price point mid-way between GS and XS types.

For 2003 and the first half of 2004 (MY), the range was cut back to five models (E,S, GS, XS and ES). From February 2004, there were just three run-out models (advertised as "Definitive Editions"). These were the Pursuit, the Landmark and the ES Premium.

No UK Series II Discovery carried model badging before February 2004. The Definitive Editions were fitted with silver-finish name badges on the tail door (although some early examples seem not to have had them).

Equipment and specification levels generally became higher as time went on.

Top models had self-adjusting air springs at the rear, which were kept inflated by a chassis-mounted pump

However, leather upholstery was only ever standard on ES models, and E and early S models always had steel disc wheels instead of alloys. Models with 255-section tyres always had wheelarch eyebrows, but those with 235-section or 205-section tyres did not. 7-seaters always had SLS.

It was of course always possible to upgrade the specification of a vehicle by adding items from the options list at the time of purchase, and many vehicles were far from "standard" when delivered to their first owners.

North American models

For MY 1999 and 2000, North America had a two-model range. The main choice was between cloth and leather upholstery; both were available with five or seven seats and various option packages, but the models with leather had a generally higher specification than those with cloth. Mid-way through the 2001 model-year, Duragrain PVC upholstery replaced the cloth option.

The 2001 model-year brought three basic models, each available with five or seven seats. Entry-level models were badged SD, and had Duragrain upholstery. The mid-range LE model had cloth-and-leather upholstery, and the top model with leather upholstery was the SE. When fitted with seven seats, these models were badged SD7, LE7 and SE7.

For the 2002 model-year, the range was cut back to two basic types, called S and SE.

The range was expanded to three models again for 2003 and 2004. Entry-level S types had Duragrain upholstery. The mid-range SE had leather, and the top-model HSE had a package of extra equipment. All were available with five or seven seats.

Special models

Commercials

"Commercial", or van derivatives of the Discovery were built by Land Rover Special Vehicles. Series I models were introduced in April 1993 and remained available until the end of Series I production. Series II types arrived in May 2001 and remained available until the end of production in 2004. Genuine Commercials have LRSV badges on tailgate and front wings. All Series Is have a decal badge; Series IIs built between 1998 and 2002 have a plastic badge, and Series IIs built in 2003-2004 have a silver-finish metal badge.

The Series I derivatives are mostly diesel-engined with manual gearboxes, and are all based on low-specification three-door models. They have the two regular front seats but behind that the whole body is given over to carrying space; the rear side windows are panelled over.

Series II Commercials are again mostly diesel manuals, with a similar interior configuration including a full-height bulkhead. Instead of sheet metal in the rear side window apertures, however, they have blackout glass. All are 5-doors, of course, and in place of the drop-glass in each rear side door is a fixed pane of blackout glass. SLS, ACE and steel wheels are standard equipment.

Some countries had their own special derivatives of the Commercial, built to meet local regulations. These included Ireland (which created its own van derivatives of both Series I and Series II models before LRSV produced the "factory" versions) and the Netherlands (where the Series I Commercials had raised roofs and were converted locally by specialist Ter Berg).

Series I Commercials were based on three-door models. This is a 300-series example

Police and special-purpose derivatives

Several UK Police Forces used Series I and Series II Discoverys as patrol vehicles, and these have mostly found their way onto the civilian market after their Police life is over. Such vehicles are usually painted white and will often have additional electrical harnesses and additional mounting brackets for Police equipment. However, there was no universal standard Police specification, as individual forces had their own preferences.

There were also some special-purpose derivatives of the Series I Discovery. These include a small number of ambulances on a 116-inch wheelbase for the UK, a small number of tipper trucks on a 3040mm (119.7 inch) wheelbase for Switzerland, and some pick-up models for Denmark. There was also a handful of wheelchair carriers with raised roofs and a chair lift at the rear, probably all sold in the UK.

Series I Special Models

Discovery sales peaked in 1996, but Land Rover had accurately predicted this and from mid-year bolstered sales with a series of limited editions in the UK. A similar pattern was followed overseas, but the special editions were created and badged to suit local market conditions. There isn't room to list all the limited editions offered worldwide, but the tables below give details of the UK and North American models. They are arranged in alphabetical order for ease of reference.

Model	Release date	Number built	Remarks
Anniversary 50	April 1998	1000	5-door 7-seater in Atlantis Blue (800 examples) or White Gold (200), with roof rails, bright rubbing strip, fog lamps and special badging on wings and tailgate. Boost alloy wheels with 235 tyres. Lightstone leather, leather steering wheel rim, air conditioning, heated windscreen, driver's airbag, top-spec ICE with CD, stainless steel tread strips, auto-dim mirror, wood trim on HVAC and leather-effect door inserts. V8 and Tdi automatics, or Tdi manual
Argyll	June 1997	600	5-door based on mid-range S model. Oxford Blue or Woodcote Green with dished alloy wheels and special badging. V8 and Tdi automatics, or Tdi manual
Argyll	April 1998	Not known	3-door 5-seater, with twin manual sunroofs, roof rails, Castor alloys on 235 tyres, front mud flaps and headlamp power wash. Argyll decals. Driver's airbag, power-adjusted and heated door mirrors. Tdi engine; manual standard with automatic optional

The Anniversary 50 was the only Discovery to have Atlantis Blue paint

Model	Release date	Number built	Remarks
Aviemore	1998	Not known	7-seater based on mid-range GS specification. British Racing Green or Rioja Red with dished alloy wheels, cloth upholstery and heated windscreen
Discovery 150	July 1996	150	5-door 5-seater with Tdi engine and manual gearbox; special edition created by a group of East Midlands dealers. Dished alloy wheels, special side graphics and badged spare wheel cover; no roof rails
Goodwood	October 1996	500	5-door in British Racing Green with coachlines, dished alloy wheels, wood trim and top-spec ICE system. Only the Motor Show car was badged as a Goodwood; the owners of the Goodwood racing circuit objected to the use of their trademark
Horse and Hound	January 1997	20	5-door special edition created by Lex Land Rover of Maidenhead, Berkshire in conjunction with Horse and Hound magazine. Based on Tdi S; special side decals; probably all Epsom Green

Model	Release date	Number built	Remarks
Safari	June 1998	1100	5-door based on GS 7-seater with twin sunroofs. Highland Green or Altai Silver with Tornado alloy wheels, chromed side runners, bright rubbing strip inserts, A-bar with fog lamps, perspex lamp protectors, rear ladder and roof rails. Leather steering wheel rim, twin airbags, air conditioning, heated windscreen, carpet protectors, loadspace mat and top-spec ICE with CD player. Safari wing badges

North American market

Model	Release date	Number built	Remarks
50th Anniversary	1998 model year	50	Based on the LSE and finished in Woodcote Green with special decals on tailgate and rear sides; Bahama Beige leather upholstery with Lightstone piping, numbered brass special edition plate on dash, special overmats, Tornado alloy wheels
LSE	1997 model year	400	Based on the SE and available in White Gold or British Racing Green (200 of each), in each case with Lightstone leather upholstery. Introduced late in the season
XD	1997 model year	275	Of the 275 built, 25 were for Canada and the remaining 250 for the USA. Ten were used in the dealer TReK competition and were badged appropriately; a further 28 were used in the Eco-Challenge. All were distinguished by AA Yellow paint and black-painted wheel centres. Automatic transmission, skidplate, lamp guards and roof rack were all standard

The 1997-model XD for North America was strikingly turned out

The Honda Crossroad

Throughout the 1980s and up until the BMW take-over in 1994, the Rover Group had a close working relationship with the Japanese Honda company. Honda wanted to break into the 4x4 market in the early 1990s, and chose to gain experience of that market first by buying in 4x4s from other manufacturers and badging them as Hondas. Among those it chose was the Discovery, which it badged as a Honda Crossroad.

The Crossroad was sold only in Japan, and never became a strong seller. Just 928 were sold between the start of sales on November 1, 1993 and the end in mid-1995. All were 5-door V8i models, and those sold in the latter part of 1994 and 1995 had the "facelift" specification of 300-series models.

Camel Trophy Discoverys

Land Rover provided the vehicles for the Camel Trophy adventure expedition while the Series I Discovery was in production, and each year Land Rover Special Vehicles (known as SVO in the earlier period) prepared a number of Discoverys for the event. Many were sold off to the public afterwards, and they have their own special following.

3-door Tdi models were used on the 1990 Camel Trophy, but 5-door Tdi models were used on the 1991-1997 events. Between 16 and 20 vehicles were prepared each year, distinctively painted in Sandglow and equipped with a rollcage, roof rack, auxiliary lighting, bull-bars and light guards.

The Series II Commercials were five-doors, with blackout glass in the rear

Series II Special Models

Special-edition Series II models were used to present attractive versions of the Discovery in specific price brackets whenever pricing action or new models from rival manufacturers looked like damaging Discovery sales. Once again, these tables are arranged in alphabetical order for ease of reference with UK market models first.

Model	Release date	Number built	Remarks
Braemar	November 2001	75	Sold through dealers in Scotland only; 7-seater Td5 in Blenheim Silver; 25 automatic and 50 manual; Play Stations, privacy glass, picnic tables; Safari 5000 lamps on black mounting bar with steady bar; front and rear lamp guards, rear ladder and side rubbing strips; 18-inch Triple Sport alloy wheels
G4 Edition	September 2003	250	Td5 manual (automatic optional) in Borrego Yellow, Tangiers Orange, Zambezi Silver or Java Black with front wing decals, body colour apron and Style 3 16-inch wheels; A-frame, front and rear lamp guards, Aero roof rails with lockable crossbars; centre differential lock, SLS, cruise control, headlamp power wash; Black Mogul fabric upholstery, air conditioning, single-slot CD player in Foundry dash insert, tool kit, first aid kit, auto-dimming rear view mirror.

Model	Release date	Number built	Remarks
Metropolis	October 2002	250	Td5 or V8, all automatic. Java Black with privacy glass to the rear and black leather upholstery; seven seats. ACE, SLS, two electric sunroofs; side bump strips with bright inserts, side runners, Style 6 18-inch wheels; driving lamps; Metropolis badges on tailgate and front wings; Harman/Kardon ICE with CD; heated windscreen; power-adjusted and heated front seats; auto-dimming rear view mirror; satnav system with Trafficmaster in roof-mounted console
Millennium (MM)	January 2000	1150, plus 290	Td5, V8 optional; ACE; seven seats; Dark Smokestone Alcantara and leather upholstery with heated front seats and two-tone leather steering wheel rim; wood on dash and doors; air conditioning and power-fold mirrors; ACE and 16-inch Lightning alloy wheels. First batch of 1150 in Blenheim Silver (275), Oxford Blue (275) or unique Carmen Pearlescent paint (600). Second batch of 290 (265 diesels, 25 V8s) built in May-June. All V8s and most Td5s with automatic transmission; painted Alveston Red, Blenheim Silver or Oxford Blue.
Serengeti	March 2002	600 (original forecast)	Td5 with five seats (seven seats with SLS optional); air conditioning and 6-speaker ICE; available in Alveston Red, Epsom Green, Java Black, Oslo Blue or Zambezi Silver; special wing badges; 18-inch ProSport alloy wheels

North American market

Model	Release date	Number built	Remarks
G4 Edition	2004 model year	200	4.6-litre engine; Tangiers Orange paint, with Aero roof rails, A-frame, lamp guards, Foundry trim finish with Black Mogul fabric upholstery; power-adjusted front seats; black leather steering wheel rim and in-dash CD player

Model	Release	Number built	Remarks
Kalahari	October 2001	150	Borrego Yellow paint; Saudi-spec grille and front apron, black brush bar and lamp guards, roof rack and rear ladder, twin electric sunroofs and 16-inch Typhoon alloy wheels. Tailgate badge with limited-edition number. Duragrain upholstery with black Tetra fabric panels and Ash Grey side bolsters; leather on cubby lid and door grab handles; Brunel trim on passenger's side of dash; 220-watt ICE with 12 speakers and CD changer
TReK	2000 model year	16	The 16 Discoverys built for the TReK dealer competition in late 1999 were not strictly a special edition, but were later sold off to the public. Molten Orange paint with TReK graphics and black 16-inch alloy wheels with 245/75R16 BF Goodrich Mud Terrains; Saudi-spec bumper and mesh grille; wrap-around brush bar, winch, four Hella driving lamps, two rear work lights, rear ladder, full-length roof rack, rock sliders, Hi-Lift jack, uprated front springs, rear lamp guards, rubber floor and cargo mats.
TReK 2000	2001 model year	15	There were 15 more Discoverys built for the TReK dealer competition in late 2000. These were essentially the same as the 1999 TRek Discoverys but had black Duragrain upholstery. Again not strictly a special edition, they were nevertheless sold off to the public after the competition was over.

The Series II models prepared for the 2000 TReK competition were later sold to the public

Production information

VIN identification

All Discoverys are identified by a VIN (Vehicle Identification Number), which consists of an 11-digit prefix code followed by a 6-digit serial number. Two different systems are used, one for NAS models and one for the rest of the world. The tables below show how to identify when any Discovery was built and (broadly) what specification it originally had. Where the abbreviation MY appears, this is based on the Land Rover model year, which normally runs from September to August, e.g. a 1990 MY could have been built between September 1989 and August 1990

GENUINE
PARTS

IMPORTANT

The VIN is on a plate mounted to the bonnet shut panel. From the start of the 1994 model-year, it was also visible through the bottom edge of the windscreen

Series I models (except North America)

A typical VIN would be SALLJGBF7GA123456. This breaks down into 10 groups, which decode as follows:

Digits in VIN	Explanation	Remarks
SA	Rover Group	
L	Land Rover	
LJ	Discovery Series 1	
G	Body code type	D = Honda Crossroad; G = Standard 100-inch wheelbase
B	Second type code	A = Commercial; B = 3-door estate body; M = 5-door estate body
F	Engine type code	F = Tdi; L = 3.5-litre injected V8; M = 3.9-litre injected V8; V = 3.5-litre carburettor V8; Y = Mpi
7	Steering and transmission code	3 = RHD automatic; 4 = LHD automatic; 7 = RHD 5-speed manual; 8 = LHD 5-speed manual
G	Model-year code (NB Not necessarily the same as calendar year of build)	G = 1990; H = 1991; J = 1992; K = 1993; L = 1994; M = 1995; T = 1996; V = 1997; W = 1998
A	Assembly location	A = Solihull
123456	Serial number	

Series I North American models

A typical North American Discovery VIN might be SALJY1240SA456789. This breaks down into nine groups, which decode as follows:

SAL	Land Rover	
JY	Model code and destination	JN = Discovery for California; JY = Discovery for other states and Canada
1	Body type	1 = 5-door
2	Engine type	2 = 3.9-litre or 4.0-litre V8
4	Gearbox type	4 = 4-speed automatic; 8 = 5-speed manual
0	Check digit	May be 0 to 9, or X
S	Model year (NB Not necessarily the same as calendar year of build)	G = 1990; H = 1991; J = 1992; K = 1993; L = 1994M = 1995; T = 1996; V = 1997; W = 1998
A	Build location	A = Solihull
45678	Serial number	

Series II models (excluding North America)

The principles behind Series II VIN codes are the same as for Series Is. A typical VIN might be SALLTGM93YA789123. This decodes as follows:

SA	Rover Group	
L	Land Rover	
LT	Series II	
G	First type code	A = Japanese models; G = Standard wheelbase
M	Body type code	M = 5-door
9	Engine type code	1 = 4.0 V8 (low compression, with catalyst); 2 = 4.0 V8 (high compression, with catalyst); 3 = 4.0 V8 (low compression, no catalyst); 7 = Td5 (EGR, no catalyst); 8 = Td5 (EGR, no catalyst); 9 = Td5 (EGR, no catalyst, for Australia, EEC and Japan)
3	Steering and transmission code	3 = RHD automatic; 4 = LHD automatic; 7 = RHD 5-speed manual; 8 = LHD 5-speed manual
Y	Model year (NB Not necessarily the same as calendar year of build)	X = 1999; Y = 2000; 1 = 2001; 2 = 2002; 3 = 2003; 4 = 2004
A	Build location	A = Solihull
456789	Serial number	

From the 1994 model-year on, all Discoverys also had the VIN visible through the windscreen, as here

Series II models (North America)

Again, the principles behind Series IIs VINs are the same as those behind Series I VINs. A typical VIN might be SALTY1240XA321987. The nine code-groups break down as follows:

SAL	Land Rover	
TY	Discovery Series II, 1999 model year	TH = 2001 MY LE 5-seater; TJ = 2001 MY LE 7-seater; TK = S or SD model with Duragrain upholstery and seven seats; TL = S or SD model with Duragrain upholstery and five seats; TM = 2000-2002 MY 5-seater; TN = 2000-2002 MY 7-seater; TP = 2003-2004 MY HSE 5-seater; TR = 2003-2004 MY HSE 7-seater; TY = either 1999 MY (all models) or 2003-2004 MY 5-seater
1	5-door body	
2	Engine type code	2 = 4.0-litre V8; 4 = 4.6-litre V8; 5 = 4.0-litre V8 to LEV standards; 6 = 4.6-litre V8 to LEV or ULEV standards
4	Transmission code	4 = 4-speed automatic
0	Check digit	May be 0 to 9, or X
X	Model-year (NB Not necessarily the same as the calendar year of build)	X = 1999; Y = 2000; 1 = 2001; 2 = 2002; 3 = 2003; 4 = 2004
A	Build location	A = Solihull
321987	Serial number	

On Series II models, the VIN plate can most easily be found on this plate on the bonnet lock platform

Year by year body colours and interior choices

This section lists the colour choices and fabrics available from year to year. The colour code sticker on a Discovery can be found on the bonnet shut platform, on the right-hand side as you look into the engine bay.

Discovery Series I (1990-94 MY)		1990	1991	1992	1993	1994
Solid colours						
Corallin Red	S/B	X	X	X	X	X
Davos White	S	X				
Eskdale Green	B		X	X	X	X
Pebblestone Beige	B		X	X		
Pennine Grey	S		X	X	X	X
Savarin White	B		X	X	X	X
Windjammer Blue	S	X	X	X	X	X
Clear over base solid colours						
Caracal Black	S/B	X	X	X	X	X
Metallic colours						
Armada Gold	B		X	X	X	X
Aspen Silver	S			X	X	X
Zanzibar Silver	S	X	X			
Micatallic colours						
Aegean Blue	S				X	X
Arken Grey	S	X	X	X	X	X
Cairngorm Brown	S			X		
Carrigada Green	B		X	X	X	X
Foxfire Red	S/B	X	X	X	X	X
Ionian Blue	S			X	X	X
Marseilles Blues	S	X	X			
Mistrale Blue	S	X	X	X		
Sonoran Brown	B				X	X

Notes for above list:
Interior trim was in Sonar Blue (S) or Bahama Beige (B) cloth. Corallin Red changed from Sonar Blue to Bahama Beige from 1991, and that Caracal Black and Foxfire Red changed from Sonar Blue to Bahama Beige from 1993.
3-door models for 1990 and 1991 had side decals with a grey background and green highlights (Armada Gold, Caracal Black, Carrigada Green, Davos White, Eskdale Green, Marseilles Blue, Pebblestone Beige, Pennine Grey, Savarin White and Zanzibar Silver) or blue highlights (Arken Grey, Corallin Red, Foxfire Red, Mistrale Blue and Windjammer Blue).
3-door models for 1992 had side decals in grey and green with a compass motif. These were optional on 1993-94 3-door models.
Notes for list on page 53: Interior colours were Bahama Beige (B) or Granite Grey (G). Granite Grey was renamed Dark Granite with the 1996 model year; at the same time all cloth trim became known as Gleneden and half-leather trim with "Land Rover" fabric was made available for XS models. 1998 models had Kestrel cloth trim.

Discovery Series I (1995-98 MY)		1995	1996	1997	1998
Solid colours					
Alpine White	B		X	X	
Aries Blue	G		X	X	
Chawton White					X
Coniston Green	B	X	X	X	
Corallin Red	B	X			
Portofino Red	B		X	X	
Rutland Red					X
Savarin White	B	X			
Windjammer Blue	G	X			
Clear over base solid colours					
Beluga Black	B		X	X	X
Caracal Black	B	X			
Metallic colours					
Altai Silver	G		X	X	X
Armada Gold	B	X			
Aspen Silver	G	X			
Charleston Green	B			X	X
Cobar Blue					X
Niagara Grey	G	X	X	X	
Riviera Blue	G			X	
White Gold					X
Willow Green	B		X	X	
Micatallic colours					
Aegean Blue	G	X			
Avalon Blue	G	X	X	X	
Biarritz Blue	G		X		
British Racing Green	B			X	X
Caprice Teal	B	X	X		
Carrigada Green	B	X			
Epsom Green	B		X	X	X
Montpellier Red	B	X			
Oxford Blue					X
Plymouth Blue	G	X			
Rioja Red	B		X	X	X

British Racing Green was available only on the special-edition Goodwood and Aviemore models.

Discovery Series I, North America, 1994-1998		1994	1995	1996	1997	1998
Solid colours						
Alpine White	B	X	X	X	X	
Chawton White	B					X
Coniston Green	B	X	X			
Portofino Red	B	X	X	X		
Rutland Red	B					X
Clear over base solid colours						
Beluga Black	B/L	X	X	X	X	X
Metallic colours						
Altai Silver	G			X	X	
Charleston Green	B				X	X
Cobar Blue	B					X
Roman Bronze	B	X	X			
White Gold	L					X
Willow Green	B/L			X	X	
Micatallic colours						
Ardennes Green	B	X				
Avalon Blue	B			X	X	
Biarritz Blue	B		X			
British Racing Green	L					X
Caprice Teal	B	X	X			
Epsom Green	B		X	X	X	X
Oxford Blue	B/L				X	X
Plymouth Blue	B	X				
Rioja Red	B			X	X	
Woodcote Green	B					X

Notes for above list

For the 1994-1997 model-years, Beige (B) interior trim was used with all colours except Altai Silver, which had Granite (G) trim. For the 1998 model-year, Lightstone Beige (L) was used on all LSE models. Exterior colours for the LSE were limited to Beluga Black, British Racing Green, Oxford Blue, White Gold and Willow Green. British Racing Green and White Gold were available only on LSE models. Note that a low-specification Discovery SD was also sold alongside the Series II models for the first few months of the 1999 model year.

Notes for listing on page 55

All paints were clear-over-base types. Carmen Pearlescent was used only on the first batch of Millennium Edition Discoverys in the 2000 model-year; it was later replaced on the limited edition by Alveston Red. A limited range of colours was available for the Adventurer model in 2001. Those NOT available were Caledonian Blue, Coniston Green, Rutland Red, Icelandic Blue, Monte Carlo Blue, Oslo Blue and Blenheim Silver.

Discovery Series II	1999	2000	2001	2002	2003	2004
Solid colours						
Belize Green					X	X
Caledonian Blue	X	X	X	X		
Chawton White	X	X	X	X	X	X
Coniston Green	X	X	X	X		
Rutland Red	X	X	X	X	X	X
Micatallic colours						
Adriatic Blue						X
Alveston Red		X	X	X	X	X
Carmen Pearlescent		X				
Epsom Green	X	X	X	X	X	X
Giverny Green						X
Icelandic Blue		X	X	X		
Java Black	X	X	X	X	X	X
Kent Green		X	X			
Kinversand	X	X	X			
Monte Carlo Blue			X	X	X	X
Oslo Blue		X	X	X	X	
Oxford Blue	X	X				
Rioja Red	X					
Vienna Green				X	X	X
Woodcote Green	X					
Metallic colours						
Blenheim Silver	X	X	X			
Bonatti Grey			X	X	X	X
Charleston Green		X				
Cobar Blue	X	X				
Helsinki Blue						X
Maya Gold						X
Niagara Grey	X	X				
White Gold	X	X	X	X	X	X
Zambesi Silver				X	X	X

Discovery Series II interiors

Dashboards and other hard interior trim were in grey on 1999-2002 models and in black on 2003-2004 models. Interior trim options were changed every two years and were as follows:
1999-2000
Cumbria and Carlisle cloth in grey or beige; Dark Smokestone or Bahama Beige leather; Lightstone leather with Bahama Beige piping (ES Premium Pack only in UK); Land Rover Oval cloth with Dark Smokestone or Bahama Beige seat side bolsters in leather (XS only in UK): Leather and alcantara in Dark Smokestone (MM limited edition only in UK)
2001-2002
Drystone and Wall cloth in grey or beige; Dark Smokestone or Bahama Beige leather, Lightstone leather with Bahama Beige piping (ES Premium Pack only in UK); Leather and alcantara in Dark Smokestone or Bahama Beige; Indiana leather and Pioneer cloth (Adventurer only in UK)
2003-2004
Cloth in Black or Tundra; Alcantara in Alpaca, Black or Tundra; Leather in Alpaca, Black or Tundra; (Tundra was not available with Belize Green, Rutland Red, Giverny Green, Monte Carlo Blue, Oslo Blue or Helsinki Blue)

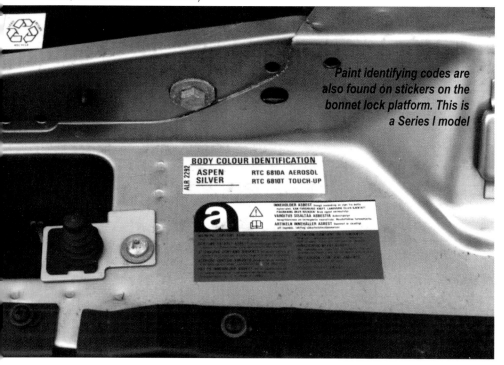

Paint identifying codes are also found on stickers on the bonnet lock platform. This is a Series I model

Discovery Series II, North America	1999	2000	2001	2002	2003	2004
Solid colours						
Chawton White	X	X	X	X	X	X
Rutland Red	X	X				
Micatallic colours						
Adriatic Blue						X
Alveston Red		X	X	X	X	X
Epsom Green	X	X	X	X	X	X
Giverny Green						X
Icelandic Blue					X	X
Java Black	X	X	X	X	X	X
Kent Green		X	X			
Kinversand	X	X				
Monte Carlo Blue					X	X
Oslo Blue			X	X	X	
Oxford Blue	X	X				
Rioja Red	X					
Vienna Green				X	X	X
Woodcote Green	X					
Metallic colours						
Blenheim Silver	X	X	X			
Bonatti Grey			X	X	X	X
Maya Gold						X
White Gold	X	X	X	X	X	X
Zambesi Silver				X	X	X

Notes for the above list
All paints were clear-over-base types.
Dashboards and other hard interior trim were in grey on 1999-2002 models and in black on 2003-2004 models.
Interior trim options were changed every two years and were as follows:
1999-2000: Cloth or leather in Dark Smokestone or Bahama Beige;
2001-2002: Duragrain PVC in Dark Smokestone or Bahama Beige; Indiana cloth in Beige with Pioneer leather in Brown; Leather in Dark Smokestone or Lightstone
2003-2004: Duragrain PVC or leather in Black or Alpaca Beige.

Options

The Discovery was all about options, right from the start. It was part of Land Rover's marketing strategy to keep the base price as low as possible, but to offer a wide range of attractive extras which would enable customers to personalise their vehicles. As many as 50 factory-fit options were available when the vehicle was launched in 1989, and their number swiftly increased.

It was part of Land Rover's policy to offer both line-fit options (such as electric front windows on early Discoverys) and dealer-fit aftermarket options (such as bull bars or side runners). Many of the items which were line-fit options on cheaper Discoverys were in fact standard on more expensive models; various combinations of line-fit options and aftermarket options were also used to create some of the special-edition models over the years.

It is therefore very nearly impossible to be certain exactly what equipment a particular Discovery would have had when it was new. The only way to find out is from the original build record (which is a rare find indeed) or from the original dealer's paperwork when the vehicle was sold new (again, a pretty rare find). Many owners added more options to their vehicles after they had owned them for a while – I've done that myself – and so the "original" specification can easily become lost over time. Most Discovery buyers really don't mind whether the options fitted to their vehicles were there when they were new; they are just grateful to have them!

Buying a used Discovery

More than 670,000 examples of the Series I and Series II Discoverys were built, which means that there are an awful lot around to choose from. It is of course very tempting to buy the very first half-decent one you see, especially if you've fallen in love with the idea of owning a Discovery and can't wait to get started. Remember, though, that if there's something not quite right about any Discovery you look at, the chances are that another, better example will turn up soon.

If you follow the advice in this section of the book, you're unlikely to make any major purchasing mistakes. However, if you're not confident about inspecting a used vehicle, take along an expert when you go to look at it, and listen to that expert's advice. It could save you big bills later.

Discovery culture

Although you'll hear people referring to the Discovery as an off-road vehicle, it is in fact a dual-purpose vehicle, suitable for both on-road and off-road use.

Most Discoverys have never been used seriously off-road, and most probably never will be. The fact is that they are such competent and practical on-road vehicles that they appeal to owners who haven't the slightest interest in getting the tyres dirty or ploughing through deep mud.

However, many Discoverys will have been modified for regular off-road use. In effect, their owners change the balance of the compromise specification which Land Rover drew up to make the Discovery such a competent all-rounder. Body lifts, chunky tyres, winches and the like can all make a Discovery into a better off-road performer, but in most cases they will also make it slightly less competent on the road. So if all you want from your Discovery is everyday road use, avoid one that has modifications like these.

If you want your Discovery to be a serious and regular off-road vehicle, all well and good. The key thing here is to reassure yourself that whatever modifications had

Introduced mid-way through the 1997 model-year, the Bodystyle Choice kit did not prove popular and is quite rare now

Series I and Series II Discoverys compared.
The Series II (left) is an early example with the original rectangular headlights.

been made to it before you bought it were done to a good standard. Also worth thinking about is whether these are the modifications you would have made if you had started with an unmodified vehicle; you may get closer to what you want if you start with a completely standard vehicle.

It's part of the Land Rover culture that vehicles get modified, and it was part of the Discovery culture from the very beginning that it should be made available with a wide range of accessories so that owners could personalise their vehicles. So don't be surprised to find anything from non-original alloy wheels to uprated engines on a Discovery that's offered for sale.

There's a second reason behind the wealth of modifications and upgrades that many owners have made to early Discoverys.

The original vehicle was quite sparsely

equipped and many vehicles have had extras added as they have passed from one owner to the next.

With the facelifted models of the 300-series era came a move up-market which was reflected in higher equipment levels. More and more Discoverys were being bought with a luxury specification which needed no additions, and subsequent buyers (in the UK, at least) have proved reluctant to hack such well-equipped Discoverys about and turn them into off-road specials. As their value drops and their condition deteriorates, however, that position is likely to change. In the meantime, entry-level Discoverys from the 300-series era still provide plenty of opportunity for radical modifications of all kinds.

By the time of the Series II models, the Discovery had been accepted into UK middle-class suburban culture as a realistic alternative to a well-specified saloon-based estate car. For this reason, most Series IIs sold in the UK had a relatively high specification. Entry-level models weren't much liked and are quite rare; even mid-range models were often kitted out from new with as many of the desirable options as the owner could afford!

As a result, major modifications to Series II models remain rare, although second and third owners have tended to add items from the options list that were not specified when the vehicle was new. However, as the vehicles become older and cheaper, it seems reasonable to expect that we will see more radical modifications, particularly for off-road use.

It was rather different in North America, where all Discoverys had equipment levels which were high by UK standards. US and Canadian owners have tended to modify their Discoverys mainly for off-road use, if at all – and that goes for both Series I and Series II models, regardless of their specification levels.

Documentation

The older the Discovery you're looking at, the more important it is to check the documentation that comes with it. A full service history is very reassuring, of course, and a definite plus – but perhaps most of all you should double-check that the VIN and engine numbers on the paperwork do tie up with those on the vehicle. For a breakdown of what the VIN numbers reveal about a vehicle, refer back to page 49.

The bolt-together construction of the Discovery means that it's not hard to build a vehicle from parts of several others, and not hard to create a "ringer". You're more likely to come across villainy with the Series I models because the greater complexity of the Series IIs is a deterrent to the back-street bodger, but don't say you weren't warned!

Rear views of Series I and II (on left)

Despite the use of aluminium for outer body panels, early Discoverys do suffer from corrosion. This is typical of the problem, and is behind the front wheelarch

The problem of corrosion is even greater when it breaks out behind the side graphics, as here. Replacements for those decals on early Discoverys are now hard to find

Chassis frame

The Series I Discoverys sit on what is essentially a classic Range Rover chassis, while the Series IIs have a further-developed version of the same ladder-frame design. Some very early Discoverys are now suffering from severe chassis corrosion, and even relatively recent Series II models will probably have surface rusting on the chassis members. Recent underseal may be just a ploy by the seller to cover up something unpleasant – so look very carefully!

Discoverys that have done a lot of off-road work may have several dings and dents in the chassis, but these need not be anything to worry about. On the other hand, you should worry about signs of plating on the chassis; it will be covering bad rust or – less likely – a serious dent.

Bodywork

Although the Series I and Series II Discoverys look very similar, the only body panel they actually have in common is the tail door. That can be a source of problems: look for corrosion in the lower corners, and listen for excessive rattling on the move. Rattles may be caused by a worn locking catch or lock linkages, or by worn hinges; you can check for all these with the vehicle static after your road test.

While Series I models have alloy outer panels (except for the roof and rear quarters), the Series IIs have steel panels. The main reason for the switch to steel was to get better panel gaps and, so far, the factory-applied protective measures have allowed Series II bodies to remain rust-free. On Series Is, however, look for aluminium corrosion, particularly in the doors and in the area behind the rear wheelarches.

Corrosion also attacks the boot floor on Series I models, and it's not uncommon to find holes or patches under the carpet. Sometimes the whole floor will be replaced, but it's often rivetted into place rather than welded. This is a sure sign that an owner has skimped on repairs and should alert you to look for other signs of neglect. Look, too, for a rusted-out body cross-member below the big tail door.

The front apron spoiler is vulnerable to damage on all Discoverys, especially if they get taken off-road. On 200-series models, the main apron itself will often be buckled or torn. The apron of 300-series Discoverys is tougher, but can crack if it hits something solid. On Series IIs, the big spoiler is not only vulnerable but also expensive to replace. That's one reason why the 2003 and 2004 models had a different spoiler, which gave better clearance off-road.

On Series I models, check the bumpers. If the black plasticised covering has peeled off and rust has started to appear, the chances are that the vehicle has been abused and neglected. The roof bars on both Series I and Series II models may lose their black outer coating, too, especially if this has been damaged by fitting the optional roof-rack cross-bars. Note that the thicker Aero style roof bars made optional on 2003 models and standardised on some models in 2004 were not much liked, and few people ordered them.

It's worth remembering, too, that the side decals applied to the first 3-door Discoverys are very hard to come by now. So if you're looking at a vehicle which is going to need

Rust can affect the seat bases of early Discoverys and, in this case, has spread to the seat pan as well. Only 3-door models had this kind of tipping seat base

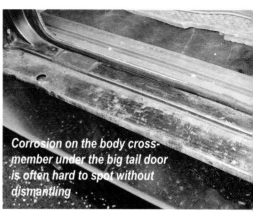

Corrosion on the body cross-member under the big tail door is often hard to spot without dismantling

Typical off-roading damage on a Series I Discovery. The sill is plastic, and can easily be replaced

a respray, remember that you might have to manage without those decals.

Lastly, 7-seater models of both the Series I and the Series II Discovery came with a self-retracting step below the rear bumper which made passenger access to the rearmost seats easier. If unused for long periods,and especially if neglected in general maintenance, these steps can seize on their mountings. You can usually free them off, but take care: it's only too easy to break something if you're brutal.

Interior

Entry-level models of both the Series I and Series II Discovery always had cloth trim, although from the 2001 model-year onwards this was replaced on NAS Series IIs by Duragrain PVC. Leather first arrived in March 1994 for top models, and was always more common on NAS Discoverys, as was the Lightstone beige leather option (known as Premium trim in the UK). Leather-and-cloth upholstery was used on XS models from 1996 on, and a different version was used on the UK-model Adventurer and the NAS LE model.

Rusted front seat bases are a sign of neglect on early models, but a generally dirty appearance need not be a cause for concern. The cloth seats usually come up well after a good clean, and dirt ingrained in the golf-ball textures of the plastic trim miraculously disappears (and quickly comes back again!). Look out, though, for damaged or torn leather trim. The leather usually wears very well, so tears are a bad sign – and are expensive to put right. On Series II models, look for signs of scuffing on the driver's seat back, where a press-stud catches it as the rear seat is folded forward.

On 300-series Discoverys, you should be aware of the "curly dash" problem. The top surface of the dashboard on the passenger's side could separate from the foam shaping underneath, usually as a result of exposure to strong sunlight, and many vehicles were dealt with under warranty. The problem can still occur, and although there are cures, it is a tricky one to put right.

In the rear of all Series Is, take a look at the side trim panels where they meet the headlining and check for signs of water leaks. Water gets in through a poor seal under the roof guttering just above the rear window. It's easy enough to stop the leak with body sealant, but it will make a mess if you don't catch it in time. In the rear of Series IIs, check the press-stud which holds the loadspace roller blind cover to the back of the rear seat. It has a tendency to pull out and will often be missing or broken.

7-seat Series I models have inward-facing rear seats. Series IIs are longer at the rear and have the optional "third row" seats facing forwards. Neither type really offers legroom for tall adults, but the Series II seating is a much better bet for regular use. It's worth knowing that 7-seaters – best suited to family buyers – are always easier to sell on than 5-seaters, and are likely to be priced slightly higher.

Don't forget to test all the electrical convenience equipment – electric windows, electric sunroofs (some vehicles have two), power-adjusted seats, and so on. These were never the most reliable components in early vehicles, and some Series II models also seem to suffer from electrical gremlins. On Discoverys which have ABS and airbags, make sure that the relevant warning lights on the dash come on with the ignition. It's easy to disguise an expensive fault by removing the warning light bulb!

On the Really Worth Having list for Series II models must be ATC, where you simply dial in the cabin temperature you want and leave the system to maintain it automatically. Driver and passenger can even dial in different temperatures and (as long as they

Wet footwell carpets like this (on a Series II) indicate that the air conditioning system's drain tubes are blocked. They can easily be rodded out from under the vehicle

Damage to the rear side trim like this can result from leaks around the guttering on Series I models

The Automatic Temperature Control system on Series II models is simple to use and extremely effective

aren't too radically different) the system will cope with their individual needs. ATC also has an excellent "fast demist" setting to clear a misted-up windscreen and, when combined with a heated windscreen, it will even shift an overnight frost very quickly.

Engines

Most Discoverys you'll come across in the UK are diesels. Series Is have 4-cylinder Tdi units (200 Tdi to 1994 and 300 Tdi thereafter); Series IIs have the 5-cylinder Td5.

There was also a V8 petrol option from the start. On 1990 models it was a 3.5-litre

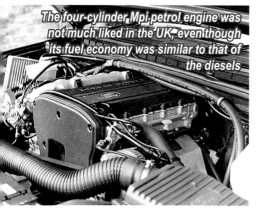

The four-cylinder Mpi petrol engine was not much liked in the UK, even though its fuel economy was similar to that of the diesels

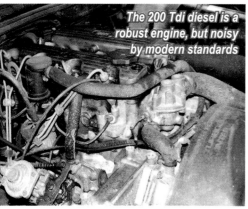

The 200 Tdi diesel is a robust engine, but noisy by modern standards

carburettor engine, from 1991-1993 it was a 3.5-litre injected type, and in 1993 it changed to a 3.9-litre injected type. From 1998, the Series II models had a 4.0-litre injected type. US and Canadian models were only ever available with V8 engines; from 1996 they had an earlier version of the 4.0-litre, and from mid-2002 they had a 4.6-litre V8.

Last and very much least was the 4-cylinder petrol "Mpi" option, available between 1992 and 1997. There aren't many around and they aren't much liked because they lack the torque of the other Discovery engines. However, the engine doesn't have any major weaknesses. Fuel economy will probably be on a par with the diesels.

The V8s should all rev freely and sound smooth. They like regular oil changes, and start to sound thrashy when neglected. Dirty oil is a sign of neglect, as is a rusty oil filter. Look out for 3.9, 4.0 and 4.6 types that lose water unaccountably; these engines can suffer from loose liners and cracked blocks (the so-called "porous block" problem). Listen, too, for rattles from defunct catalytic converters; you won't enjoy the bill for replacement.

While these are wonderful and long-lived engines, they will never give good fuel economy. Expect 14 mpg from a carburettor 3.5, and up to about 18 mpg from the others. That's why so many have been converted to LPG – and if one you're looking at has been gassed, remember that there are good conversions and bodged conversions.

As for the diesels, the older 200 Tdi is in some ways a more robust engine than the 300 Tdi which followed it, but the 300 Tdi is very much quieter. Both offer the same power and torque (although late 300 Tdi engines with automatic transmissions had a little more of each). Both have a belt-driven camshaft, and regular cambelt changes are essential; 60,000 miles is the recommended maximum between changes and expensive things can happen if the work isn't done.

On some 300 Tdi engines, the cambelt could work its way forwards over pulleys and idlers and chafe against the timing cover – which resulted in premature belt failure. Land Rover provided modification kits to prevent this happening, and most engines will have been dealt with by now. The "problem" engines were those fitted to Discoverys with VINs in the ranges MA 081991 to TA 200000, MA 500000 to VA 558898, and TA 700000 to VA 748935. Not every engine in these ranges needed modification, however and there were two different kits – one for earlier engines and one for later types. If in doubt, consult a Land Rover specialist.

The Td5 in the Series II models is smoother, quieter and altogether much more car-like than the Tdi diesels. Many traditionalists are suspicious of it, not least because it relies on electronic management, but in fact it is turning out to be a long-lived and robust engine, if less of a DIY dream than the others. It's reassuring to know that it has a chain-driven camshaft which does not need the regular attention that the Tdi engines' belt-driven types require.

One weakness of early Td5 engines is oil contamination of the injector harness, which causes erratic running but is fortunately fairly easy to fix. In some cases, oil can work its way up the harness into the engine ECU itself, but it is usually possible to dry out an oiled-up ECU successfully. Cylinder heads can also crack, and on engines built within

The later 300 Tdi diesel is a quieter engine but gained something of a reputation as a result of cambelt problems

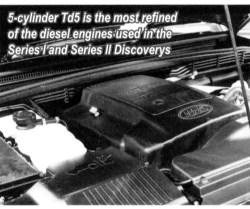

5-cylinder Td5 is the most refined of the diesel engines used in the Series I and Series II Discoverys

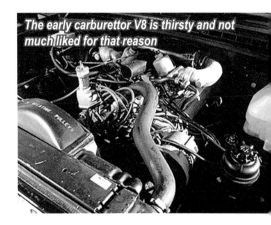

The early carburettor V8 is thirsty and not much liked for that reason

a specific period it's possible for the oil pump securing bolt to fail. The resulting mess usually demands engine replacement.

Many owners have uprated the engines of their Discoverys to improve acceleration. Typically, this is done by means of "chipping" – fitting a modified electronic chip to the engine management ECU. On engines without electronic control systems, performance improvements can also be achieved, often by changing the camshaft (on V8s) or by fitting a bigger intercooler and turning up the fuelling (on Tdi diesels).

It's important to realise that the really important change that chipping and other tuning methods bring about is to the torque of the engine, as it is this which affects the acceleration it delivers. Power increases usually come as part of the package, but they are far less important as they have a minimal effect on the top speed of a heavy and unaerodynamic vehicle like the Discovery. So don't be seduced by talk of big power out-puts, but try to find out how much the torque of a modified engine has been increased!

In many cases, boosting an engine's torque makes the vehicle more driveable and can actually reduce fuel consumption. This is particularly the case with diesels. However, using the additional performance all the time will, quite logically, result in bigger fuel bills. Remember, too, that some of the more extreme performance increases – particularly on diesels – are accompanied by less efficient combustion, with the result that the vehicle will not meet exhaust emissions regulations.

There's also a limit to what can be done on Series II Td5 models with automatic transmission. The torque capacity of the 4-speed ZF gearbox is lower than that of the R380 5-speed manual, and there's an electronic warning system built-in which will protect the gearbox and warn you before you do any damage to it. If the torque limit is approached, the electronics cause the auto selector readout on the instrument panel to flash. As the only way to stop it is to turn the engine off, you don't want to see this happening on a modified Discovery you are planning to buy!

Transmission

All Discoverys have variants of the LT230 gear-driven transfer gearbox. Early models have the LT230T and later Series Is the quieter LT230Q; Series IIs have the LT230SE. None of these derivatives has any particular vices. However, it's always worth checking that the high-low range selector operates correctly (if unused, it can seize) and that the centre differential lock does work. Series II Discoverys before 2002 didn't have a centre diff lock, relying instead on 4-wheel Electronic Traction Control, and it was only optional on later models. In the UK, most buyers thought it was an option they could do without, so they saved their money and made the centre diff lock a bit of a rarity. In North America, however, it was standardised on the final 4.6-litre models.

The original 5-speed LT77 manual gearbox could be very baulky when cold, and the approved remedy was to fill it with automatic transmission fluid. The problem lay in the synchromesh components, and Land Rover improved these to deliver the LT77S in 1991. Both gearboxes can suffer from poor internal lubrication, bu the symptoms of this are usually pretty obvious.

The R380 manual gearbox that replaced the LT77S in 1994 had a bad start in life, and by 1996 stories of warranty replacements were legion. However, it has proved to be a long-lived and reliable component, and is nothing to cause concern.

Automatic gearboxes first appeared in 1992 with V8s, and became available with diesels a year later. They were never offered with the Mpi engine. Discoverys have always had a 4-speed automatic made by ZF, which has an excellent reputation and is trouble-free – as long as oil and filter changes are made at the recommended intervals. It gives smooth changes, so any roughness warns of trouble.

Suspension and steering

The long-travel coil springs fitted to all Discoverys allow for plenty of body roll, which some people find alarming. For this reason, anti-roll bars became available in 1992, initially in the Freestyle Choice wheel-and-tyre option package. They were standardised on the 300-series and could of course be retro-fitted.

Series II models had their coil springs supplemented by an extremely effective active ride system at the front, which is called ACE (Active Cornering Enhancement). Top-spec models also had air springs at the rear to provide self-levelling and a height-adjustment feature which is useful when hitching a trailer.

The various locating arms used in the suspension depend on rubber bushes, and the biggest problem you're likely to encounter is wear in these. Worn bushes cause a vehicle to wander on the road, and in bad cases will allow the suspension components

Rubber bushes in the suspension can wear and cause the vehicle to wander. These new bushes are in a front radius arm from a 200-series Discovery

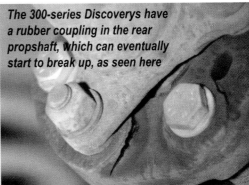

The 300-series Discoverys have a rubber coupling in the rear propshaft, which can eventually start to break up, as seen here

to knock and clunk. Replacement is time-consuming, but very worthwhile!

The worst problem in the steering, which was always power-assisted, is likely to be a worn damper. If the Discovery you're looking at suffers from bad steering wheel shake after going over a bump, the chances are that the steering damper needs replacement. It's a DIY job, and not expensive.

A dirty, battered tail door trim and additional retaining screws suggest that this early Discovery has led a hard life

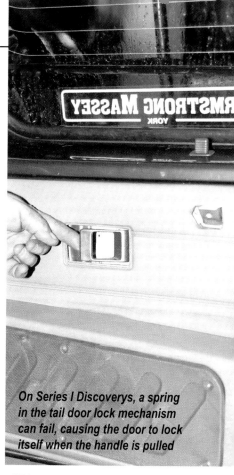

On Series I Discoverys, a spring in the tail door lock mechanism can fail, causing the door to lock itself when the handle is pulled

Brakes, wheels and tyres

All Discoverys have power-assisted disc brakes on all four wheels, and from the 1995 model year the front discs were ventilated. On Series IIs, braking revisions made for the 2003 and 2004 models gave a much more reassuring feel to the pedal – which is most noticeable if you compare one of these vehicles to an earlier Series II.

On all models, the handbrake operates on the transmission output shaft, and not on the rear wheels. This unnerves those new to Discoverys (and to most other Land Rovers) as it allows the vehicle to move slightly after the handbrake has been applied.

ABS was available on top models in the 300-series era and was standard on Series IIs. Despite a 2004 recall after a scare over leaking ABS modulators, the system doesn't usually give any trouble. Check, though, that the ABS warning light on the dash comes on with the ignition (as a system check) and then goes out once the engine has started (Series IIs) or after you've reached 5 mph (Series Is). If not, there's a problem. The ABS system is also used by the ETC when that is fitted, and by the Hill Descent Control and Electronic Brakeforce Distribution fitted to Series II models. As long as these functions work, there is no cause for concern.

Wheels have always been an important element of the Discovery's style, and even the earliest models had specially styled steel wheels. Thereafter, Land Rover introduced a wide variety of alloys, and there are now many aftermarket types on the market as well. This has persuaded many owners to update the appearance of their Discoverys with new wheels and tyres. Watch out, though, when buying second-hand: the cost of new wheels and tyres means that some owners only buy a set of four, leaving a non-matching spare concealed under the spare wheel cover!

It's worth knowing that the wheels used on Series II Discoverys will not fit Series I models, and vice versa. Other than that, three points are worth making. The first is that steel wheels are best for off-roading, as they are less prone to damage. The second is that the larger-diameter wheels (18-inch types from Land Rover and bigger ones from aftermarket suppliers) are much more vulnerable to damage when off-roading because there is correspondingly less tyre rubber to protect them. The third is that damaged alloys look awful, and are expensive to replace.

As for tyres, the standard road-biased tyres supplied by the factory are exactly that; they will cope with light off-roading but are likely to give poor performance in mud. If you want to use your Discovery off-road a lot, get a set of proper off-road tyres. The very best option is to have one set for the road (perhaps on smart alloy wheels) and another set for off-roading (perhaps on steel wheels).

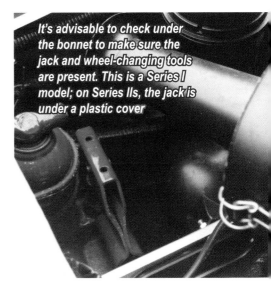

It's advisable to check under the bonnet to make sure the jack and wheel-changing tools are present. This is a Series I model; on Series IIs, the jack is under a plastic cover

For club types

There are many off-road driving clubs in the countries where the Discovery was sold, and most of these will welcome a keen Discovery owner. The exceptions, as you might expect, are those clubs devoted to a specific make of vehicle, such as Jeep or Suzuki!

The Discovery also has its own one-make club, which (not surprisingly) is called the Discovery Owners' Club. Based in the UK, the DOC nevertheless welcomes owners from all over the world. Contact details appear regularly in the 4x4 specialist magazines, and the DOC has its own web site: www.discoveryownersclub.com

To find other clubs' web sites, just type "Land Rover clubs" or "Off-road clubs" into your internet search engine.

About the author

James Taylor

James Taylor has written widely on auto-motive subjects in magazines and is the author of a number of highly-regarded motor-ing books. However, the Land Rover and Rover marques have always been his first love and specialisation, and he is currently Editor of *LAND ROVER enthusiast* magazine.

He has owned several Rover and Land Rover products, and thinks that the most satisfying of all is probably his current 2000-model Discovery Series II.

Acknowledgements

Special thanks are due to the Press Offices of Land Rover UK and Land Rover North America for a constant supply of valuable information and photographs and for a stream of Discoverys to try out over the years.

Many photographs used in this book have come from *LAND ROVER enthusiast* magazine, and thanks go to those who took them (Martin Hodder, Simon Hodder, Dave Barker, Kevin Girling and Alisdair Cusick) and to Paul Newman for retrieving the scans of them from his archive

Other titles in the Ultimate Buyers' Guide range include:

Porsche 911SC 1977 to 1983,
ISBN 0 9545579 0 5
Porsche 911 Carrera 3.2 1983 to 1989,
ISBN 0 9545579 1 3
Porsche 911 Carrera (964) 1989 to 1994,
ISBN 0 9545579 3 X
Porsche 911 Carrera (993) 1993 to 1998,
ISBN 0 9545579 2 1
Porsche Boxster & Boxster S 1996 to 2004,
ISBN 0 9545579 4 8
Porsche 911 Carrera, Turbo & GT (996),
ISBN 0 9545579 5 6
MGF and TF,
ISBN 9545579 6 4

And watch out for new titles!